RSPB Children's Guide to
BIRD
WATCHING

David Chandler and Mike Unwin

A&C Black • London

for birds
for people
for ever

The authors would like to thank the following people: Mark Boyd and Peter Carroll for expert advice; Nigel Redman, for getting the ball rolling; Julie Bailey, for editorial energies and expertise; and Sam South for making the book look as good as it does.

David Chandler would also like to thank Ruth, for understanding, Amy and Riley, for their consultancy, and Kate, for being Kate.

Mike Unwin would also like to thank his parents, for getting him started, and Kathy, for help and wise words throughout.

For A, K and F.

First published 2005 by A&C Black Publishers Ltd., 38 Soho Square, London W1D 3HB. Second edition published 2007.

Copyright © 2005 text by David Chandler and Mike Unwin.
Copyright © 2005 artwork by Hilary Burn, Alan Harris, Peter Hayman, Dave Nurney, Jim Robins, Laurel Tucker and Dan Zetterström (see full artists' credits on page 128).
Copyright © 2005 photographs (see full photographers' credits on page 128).

ISBN: 978-0-7136-8795-8

A CIP catalogue record for this book is available from the British Library.

A&C Black uses paper produced with elemental chlorine-free pulp, harvested from managed sustainable forests.

w w w . a c b l a c k . c o m

Designed by Sam South.
Printed in China by 1010 Printing International Ltd.

10   9   8   7   6   5   4   3   2

Contents

Welcome to the world of birding! 4
An introduction from Nick Baker

What is birding? 5
What this book is about and what's in it

Identification 6
Tips and techniques that help you put names to birds

Feathers 12
What they do, how they grow and what they're called

The kit 14
Choosing and using binoculars, field guides and notebooks

Habitats 22
Getting the best out of different birding habitats

Where to go 30
Finding good places to see birds

Birding action 34
How to get better views of birds

Making it count 40
Collecting information and taking part in surveys

The birder's year 44
Birding ideas for every month, with extra tips for school holidays

On your travels 50
How to see birds on a family holiday

Taking it further 52
More things you can do to enjoy birds

Useful information 54
Organisations, books, websites and bird food suppliers

Field guide 56
All you need to identify over 130 UK species

Glossary 126

Index of species 128

Welcome to the world of birding!

● ● ● ● ● ● ────────────────────

And congratulations on getting this book!

The variety of bird life is amazing. There are nearly 10,000 different species around the world, and many can be seen on our own doorstep – from the enormous Mute Swan to the tiny Goldcrest. Some, such as Kingfishers, are beautifully coloured. Others, such as Snipe, are brilliantly camouflaged. Many are capable of amazing feats: Puffins can dive deep under the ocean, geese can fly as high as jet airliners and Swifts can spend three years on the wing without landing once!

The great thing about birding is that anyone can do it. One of the best ways to get started is to spend time with someone who knows more about birds than you do. But they're not always easy to find – so that's where this book comes in.

This book can be your 'birding friend'. Its two authors have been birding for a long time. They remember what it was like to be a beginner, so they know exactly what problems you might come across. Take their advice, and you'll soon become an ace birder yourself.

When you're not reading the book, get out and see some birds. Then, maybe you can be a 'birding friend' for someone else.

Have fun!

Nick Baker
**President of RSPB Wildlife Explorers
and BBC *Really Wild Show* presenter**

What is birding?

Different people enjoy birds in different ways. Some travel the world to see as many species as possible. Others watch their local birds, or just those that visit their garden. Some watch birds on their own, some with friends and some in bigger groups. You can watch birds, study birds, draw birds, photograph birds, write about birds and put rings on birds! Some people call it bird watching, others call it birding, but the fact is there are many, many ways to enjoy birds.

Curlew

You're not alone

If you're reading this, you probably already like birds. You may not know many other people who do, but there are plenty, including young people. You are likely to meet other bird fans as you go along – it's a great way of making new friends!

Using the book

This book is divided into two parts to help you get the most out of your birding. The first part will help you with some of the skills you need to enjoy birds to the full. The second part is a guide to the birds you are most likely to see first – the common and more obvious species. Put them together and you have the perfect short cut to being a better birder.

Grey Wagtail

HOOKED!

A little interest in birding can easily become a lifelong passion. Watching birds can be exciting, challenging, relaxing and rewarding. It can change the way you see places you know, and can take you to new places. You may become hooked on other wildlife too, like butterflies, dragonflies or bats, so watch out!

You can watch birds however you like, wherever you like – it's up to you. But most of all, have fun, because the best birder is the one who enjoys it the most.

Identification

Most people want to know the name of the bird they are looking at. Some birds are easy to identify; some are not. When you start birding, trying to put the right name to a bird can be difficult and confusing. You will probably get some wrong, but don't give up. It gets easier and, with practice, you will get more of them right. Collect as many clues about the bird as you can.

Size

Bird books give birds' lengths in centimetres. Imagine the bird lying flat on its back. Its length is measured from the tip of the bill, over the top of the head and down the back, all the way to the tip of the tail. But that's not how you see birds in the wild.

The lengths in books help you to work out whether one species is bigger than another – but remember that they include the bill and tail. Long-tailed Tits are tiny birds, but because of their long tail, their length in a book suggests that they are as big as Great Tits.

Great Tits (above) and Long-tailed Tits (left) are not the same size, even though the books say they are!

You can't see centimetres when you look at a living, wild bird. So, instead, compare the bird's size to a species you know – if possible, one you can see at the same time (e.g. "about the size of a Blackbird"; "pigeon-sized"; "smaller than a Starling").

TOP TIPS

Take care if the sun is behind the bird. The edges of the bird will be less visible and the bird will look smaller and darker than it really is.

Watch out, especially in cold weather, for birds with fluffed-up feathers – they will look bigger than they are normally.

Compare the shape of your mystery bird with a bird you know. Is it like a sparrow? A pigeon? A duck? This will help you get to the right part of the field guide and makes identification easier.

Some bird shapes: Swallow, wader, pigeon, thrush, duck, gull, sparrow.

Make a note of obvious features or striking colours. Then, try to

Colour and markings

describe the whole bird from head to tail, including upperparts, underparts, bill and legs. Use the labels on pages 12–13 to help you. Be patient – you might not see everything without waiting and watching. These words will help too:

wing-bar: an obvious mark across a closed wing, or along an open wing. When a Ringed Plover flies, you can see its white wing-bar.

moustache or moustachial stripes: stripes starting near the beak and going down the bird's 'face'. Male Reed Buntings in summer plumage have a white moustache.

bars or barring: lines going across a bird's plumage. A Sparrowhawk has barring on its underparts.

streaks or streaking: lines along (not across) a bird's plumage. A Meadow Pipit has streaks on its breast and flanks.

window: a pale area, usually found on the front edge of a bird's primaries. Normally used in descriptions of gulls. Herring Gulls have white windows.

fingers: the spread feathers of a bird's wing-tips in flight, which look like fingers. You can often see fingers on Buzzards.

speculum: a bright patch of colour on a duck's wing. The male Mallard has a shiny blue speculum.

Colour confusion

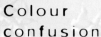

Colours don't always look the same, or the same as the picture in the field guide. The direction and brightness of the sun can change a bird's appearance. If a bird has been feeding in the mud, it might be hard to see its colours – especially on its legs and beak. Old feathers, which have been out in the wind, rain and sun for up to a year, might look paler than fresh, unworn feathers and their coloured tips may have worn off.

Some good field marks:
Woodpigeon – white
wing flash; male Bullfinch –
red breast and black cap; male Blackcap – black cap;
Redwing – rusty flanks and creamy eyebrows.

Behaviour Look at what the bird is doing and how it is moving. Does it hop, walk or run? Does it fly along in a straight line or fly up and down in a wiggly line? Does it flap all the time, or glide? What a bird does can give you important clues. In the UK, a bird hovering by a motorway is almost certainly a Kestrel (though Buzzards sometimes hover for short periods of time). Nuthatches climb up and down tree trunks – Treecreepers only climb up them.

The sounds birds make can tell you a lot. Chiffchaffs and Willow Warblers look almost the same, but their songs are completely different. You might think bird songs are too hard to learn. But make the effort to learn some of the easier ones – it will change and improve your birding. Once you know most common bird calls, an unusual one will stand out.

Treecreeper. Climbs up the trunk only.

Recordings can be helpful and there are lots to chose from (see page 55). There is even special software for loading onto an MP3 player. But the best way to learn bird song is to hear it for real, find the bird that's making the noise and identify it. Birding with someone who already knows some bird songs can be useful, too.

TOP TIP

Cup your hands behind your ears and listen. Noises coming from in front of you will sound louder.

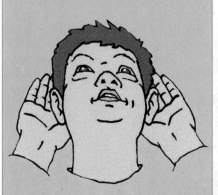

Try using words to describe songs you hear – or try drawing them (see diagram above). Remember that not all the noises birds make come from their beaks. Woodpigeons and Nightjars clap their wings together; Great and Lesser Spotted Woodpeckers drum with their beaks on trees; and breeding Snipe make a wonderful bleating noise by diving through the air with some tail feathers sticking out!

If your field guide has maps, use them to find out where the bird lives. There are no Lesser Spotted Woodpeckers in the north of Scotland. If you see a black-and-white woodpecker there it has to be a Great Spotted. Take care though. Maps can be small and it's hard to see exactly where a bird's range finishes. Some may be out of date, too – bird ranges change, though not normally very quickly.

Not all the birds you see are with us all the time. Some are here just in summer, some just in winter. Some are 'passage visitors' – they stop here on their way to somewhere else. They are 'on passage' and don't breed or spend the winter here.

Natural habitat

Migrating birds can turn up anywhere, but you'll normally find birds in their natural habitat. Use habitat information to help you identify birds. Cormorants and Shags look similar. But if you see a Cormorant-shaped bird inland, a long way from the sea, it's not likely to be a Shag.

Cormorants used to be found only on the coast. Now they're often seen inland.

TOP TIPS

If you are birding somewhere new, before you go find out which birds you are likely to see and what they look like.

If you are trying to decide whether you've seen a common bird or a rare one that looks very similar, it's probably the common one.

The most reliable identifications are based on more than one feature. Look for as many features as possible.

Taking notes

When you find a bird that you can't identify, notes (or photos, see 'Start digiscoping', page 53) will help you remember what you see. Making a simple sketch and using a few words to describe the bird is a good way to do this. You don't need to be a good artist. Even if the sketch doesn't look like the bird, it will help you remember what you saw.

Note down as much information as possible. Don't forget to record the date, place, time and weather. But concentrate on the bird first – you can do these other bits after the bird has gone. Sketching and describing a bird is a skill. You will get better at it. It makes you look hard at the bird, which helps to build up your skills.

Learn to turn eggs into birds. This is a great way to create simple bird shapes for sketches.

These egg shapes help make up simple outlines of a duck, a sparrow and a heron.

Using your bird book

Use your field guide when you are out birding – don't keep it at home. A good guide can help you work out what you should look for, to be sure of your identification. But take care not to 'see' things that aren't really there, just so you match the description in the book. And try not to spend all your time looking in the book – the bird might fly off!

Getting going

Putting names to birds is enjoyable and challenging. When you start, it's not easy. If you don't see a bird well, identification will be difficult. Don't give up. The more you practise, the better you will get. Going birding with someone more experienced can help, but don't just let them tell you the birds' names. Ask them how they know. Try to work out the birds for yourself; your skills will improve faster. Identification is just the beginning. When you know what the bird is, then you can begin to find out more about it.

Sketching wild birds will help you get to know them much better.

Feathers

Birds are the only animals with feathers. Feathers help birds to fly, control their temperature, attract a mate and hide from predators. Knowing more about feathers will also help you to identify birds.

How feathers grow

It may be hard to tell, but feathers grow from distinct areas on a bird's body – they don't grow evenly over the whole body surface. Feathers overlap one another, a bit like roof tiles. This streamlines a bird for flight and helps to keep the wind and rain out. All of the feathers put together make up a bird's plumage.

Feathers grow out of the bird's skin and, like hair or fur, are dead when fully grown. They get worn and damaged easily and are replaced at least once a year. New feathers grow and push out the old ones. This is called moult. Most birds replace all of their feathers once a year after they have bred. Some replace some of their feathers before the breeding season, too.

When you look at a bird, apart from its bill and legs, most of what you see is feathers. Knowing the names of the different feather groups makes describing a bird easier. The pictures on these two pages show the most important feather groups, as well as other parts of a bird's body. See page 7 for more bird words.

crown

forehead

beak or bill (they mean the same thing)

ear-coverts (or cheek-patch)

nape (the back of the neck)

mantle

chin

throat

scapulars (these cover the area where the wing joins the body)

breast

back

coverts (small wing feathers, covering the bases of the flight feathers)

rump

uppertail-coverts

tail

flank

undertail-coverts   vent

belly

tertials

these are the flight feathers

secondaries

primaries

leg

primaries – the long flight feathers attached to the 'hand' of the wing

secondaries – the shorter flight feathers attached to the 'arm' of the wing. The ones nearest the bird's body are called tertials.

lesser coverts – the smallest coverts

median coverts – middle-sized coverts

greater coverts – the biggest coverts

alula – very small feathers that are raised up to smooth the air flow and stop a bird falling out of the air when it is landing

primary coverts – the coverts over the bases of the primaries

eyebrow or supercilium (a stripe over the eye)

lores (the area between the base of the bill and the eye)

eye-stripe (a stripe through the eye)

moustache/moustachial stripe

Below left: A lot of the yellow in a Greenfinch wing is on the edges of the primaries.
Below right: White tips on a Coal Tit's coverts make two wing-bars.

13

The kit

You can enjoy birds without any equipment, but there are a few things you will need if you really want to get involved. The basic kit is binoculars, a field guide and a notebook.

Binoculars

For finding birds and seeing them better

Not all binoculars (or 'bins') are good for watching birds. Read this before you buy. If someone else is buying binoculars for you, get them to read this first.

Good birding binoculars:

- are not too heavy. You might be wearing them all day. Heavy bins are difficult to hold steady too.

- feel comfortable in your hands.

- have eyepieces that fold close enough together for you to see one circle when you look through them, without black shapes appearing.

- are clear and bright when you look through them.

- focus easily – focusing should be smooth and not too stiff. Try them on something close and something far away. If you want to look at butterflies or dragonflies, make sure they focus down to about two metres or less.

- don't need to cost too much.

What the numbers mean

Two numbers are used to describe binoculars. For example 8x32, or 10x42. The first number is the magnification – how many times bigger the bird will look. 8x32 binoculars magnify eight times. The second number is the diameter (width) of the big lenses at the front (the objective lenses). 10x42s have 42mm objectives. Bigger objectives let in more light and give a brighter image. Binoculars that magnify seven or eight times, and have objectives that are 30–42mm wide are very good for birding. Magnifications up to ten times are OK, but are harder to hold steady.

Compacts

If you find full-size binoculars too big to hold, try compacts. These are smaller and lighter than standard bins. They have objective lenses of less than 30mm. They may not be as bright to look through, but many give a view that is fine for birding. If you have small hands, compacts may be a good way to get started. Choose a magnification of seven or eight times.

Adjustable eyepiece

Eyecups

Focusing wheel

Objective lens

PORRO PRISMS

ROOF PRISMS

COMPACTS

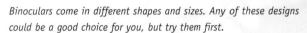

Binoculars come in different shapes and sizes. Any of these designs could be a good choice for you, but try them first.

Waterproof?

Not all binoculars are waterproof. Try to get a rainguard. This will keep the worst of the weather off the eyepieces. It protects the lenses from crumbs when you eat your lunch too! If it rains hard, tuck your binoculars inside your coat to keep them dry.

Smart shopping

If you can, buy from a specialist binocular shop with staff that know about birding. The UK bird watching links website (see pages 52 and 55) will give you some ideas of where to shop, or you can look at adverts in

Above: Using a rainguard.

birding magazines (see page 52). Decide how much you can spend, and look at a small number of binoculars that you can afford. You can get good binoculars without spending too much money, especially if you buy second-hand. Get the best you can afford. The easier they are to use, and the better the image you see through them, the more you will enjoy birding.

Strapping up

Put the strap on your binoculars and hang them around your neck. Always use the strap – it will stop you dropping your binoculars. Make sure the strap isn't too long – they should hang just below your chest. You can buy elasticated straps that are slightly 'bouncy'. These are more comfortable and make binoculars feel lighter.

Setting your sights

Your right eye may be different to your left eye, so your binoculars need to be set up to suit them both. One eyepiece will be adjustable – normally the right one. Different binoculars are adjusted in different ways. Keep both eyes open when you make adjustments.

1. Cover the right-hand objective with one hand. Use the central focusing to focus the left side on something with a clear outline 50–100m away – a chimney pot or TV aerial maybe.

Above and left: Binoculars give a great view of this Jay.

2. When the left-hand side is focused, cover up this side and use the eyepiece adjustment to focus the right side. When that side is clear, make a note of the number on the dial and keep this eyepiece set there whenever you use the binoculars.
3. Now all you need to do is use the central focusing for any bird you are looking at – however near or far away it is.

Glasses

If you wear glasses you may need to wear them when you are using binoculars (not everyone has to). To use binoculars with glasses you need to adjust the eye-cups. If the eye-cups are rubber, fold them down. If they are plastic, twist or push them down. Try it out when you buy the binoculars to make sure it works for you.

Practice makes perfect

When you are birding keep your binoculars around your neck, not inside their case. You might find it hard to find birds with your binoculars that you can see with your

naked eyes. Keep your eyes on the bird and bring your binoculars up to your eyes. If you find it difficult, practise when you're not birding – on different things around your garden maybe.

Learn which way to turn the focusing wheel to focus on more distant birds or closer ones – you don't want to waste time doing this when you're trying to look at an exciting bird! Practise focusing quickly – you could do this in the garden, too.

Above: Adjust the eyepiece to get the clearest view.

Handle with care

Protect your binoculars from bumps. Keep the lenses clean but don't clean them too often. Every time you clean them you risk scratching them. When you clean them, blow on the lenses first to get rid of crumbs, dust and sand. Lens tissues or lens cloths are the best things to clean the lenses with.

Below: Don't use your binoculars just to look for birds you've already seen. Search for birds with them too.

For identifying birds and learning more about them

A field guide is a book that has been designed for use indoors or out ('in the field'). A good field guide will help you put the right names to the birds you see and tell you something about them. The words and pictures will tell you what different birds look like, where and when you might see them and how common they are. They even tell you what sounds birds make, though these can be hard to describe (see page 9). Your field guide will help you to tell males from females, young birds from adults and birds in breeding plumage from birds in non-breeding plumage.

Good guides

There are many different field guides. Some are very good, others are not. Field guides that contain only photos are not normally as useful as those with illustrations. It's hard to get photos that show all the different features of each bird. To get you started, this book includes a field guide to the birds you are most likely to see when you start birding (see pages 56–125). Sooner or later though, you will need a guide that describes more birds than we could fit in this book. We recommend three good ones:

Recommendation 1 – for more detail

RSPB Handbook of British Birds covers the 280 most common birds in the UK – so you won't get confused by other European species. It includes lots of information about how birds live – much more than most field guides.

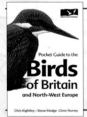

Recommendation 2 – for more birds

Pocket Guide to the Birds of Britain and North-West Europe covers 380 species, including most European species. It's the most compact of the three recommended guides and helps if you go on holiday to other parts of Europe.

Recommendation 3 – for even more birds

Collins Bird Guide covers over 700 species – all of the birds of the UK and Europe. Many people think this is the best field guide. It is very good, but all those species might confuse you when you are first learning your birds.

In really good field guides, such as the three guides on the left and Birds of Europe by Lars Jonsson (above), the words, pictures and maps for a species can all be seen at the same time. This makes the book easier to use. Field guide maps tell you where each species can be seen at different times of the year.

Left and below: Real birds vary, and don't always look exactly like their paintings in a book. And paintings can vary from one book to another. Compare these two field guide illustrations of Fulmars with the real birds in the photo above.

Remember also that a photo can make a bird look darker or paler, depending on the light. Try to use a combination of pictures and other clues to help get your identification right.

Get book-wise!

Make the most of your field guide:

● Read the introduction. It will explain the key features of *your* guide, and how to use them.

● Look through your field guide as often as you can at home. Get to know the names of the birds and what they look like.

● Learn where in the book to find different birds. Most bird books have the birds in more or less the same order. This is the order used by scientists. We have used it in this book's field guide.

● Don't worry about the book getting creased or dirty. It's a tool to be used. Use it at home and when you are out birding. Scribble notes in it, if you like.

● Most birders have more than one field guide, so that they can compare different descriptions and pictures of the same bird.

● You can install field guide software on a PDA or MP3 player. They're easy to carry when you're out bird watching, and you can hear what birds sound like, too. There are also DVD-ROMs to use at home.

A birding notebook

So you don't forget!

You don't have to use a notebook – not all birders do. But notebooks are a good way of recording what you see and making notes about birds you can't identify. If you don't record things on the spot you will quickly forget. Your notes don't have to be just for the 'science' of birding. You can jot down how birds make you feel, or even what you had for lunch! Notebooks are good for reading later, too. You can look back and remember great days out birding, months or even years later. It can also help you build up a picture of your birding and let you see how the birds in the places you go change throughout the year.

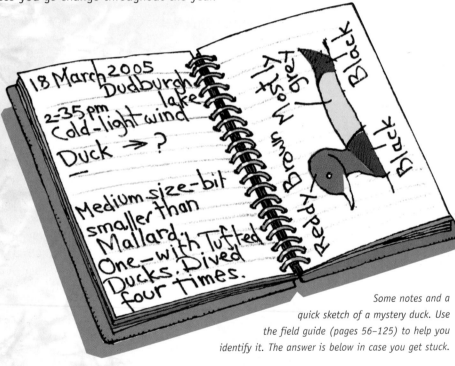

Some notes and a quick sketch of a mystery duck. Use the field guide (pages 56–125) to help you identify it. The answer is below in case you get stuck.

Take note

A good birding notebook:

- fits in your pocket

- is tough enough to stay in one piece even after lots of birding trips

- has a cover hard enough for leaning on

- opens flat enough to be easy to write in.

Answer: *The mystery duck is a Pochard.*

You can use a pencil or a pen to take notes. Some notebooks have special pen holders. Others have spiral binding you could keep your pen in. Elastic bands make good bookmarks and stop the pages flapping around.

When you have finished a notebook, remember not to throw it out – even if you think it's rubbish. Birders like looking back over their old notebooks. Their first ones are particularly special.

Write and draw things in your notebook when you are out bird watching.

Be creative

You can do whatever you like in your notebook. If you like writing, make notes about what birds do and what their colours remind you of. Use your notes back home to help you write a story or poem. If you like art, draw or paint wild birds in different positions and doing different things. You could even enter 'AllWrite' or 'WildArt', competitions organised by RSPB Wildlife Explorers.

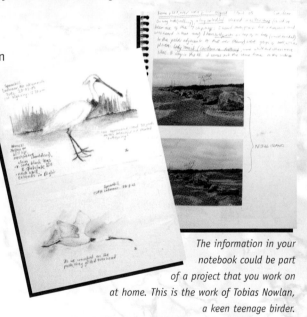

The information in your notebook could be part of a project that you work on at home. This is the work of Tobias Nowlan, a keen teenage birder.

Alternative records

Instead of a notebook, you could try:

- a checklist (a printed list of bird species, like the one inside the back cover of this book). Just tick off the ones you see, or record your counts of different species.

- a mobile phone. Make notes on it, and set the alarm so you remember to look at them later, or e-mail them to yourself! If you have a cameraphone, and a telescope, you can use your phone to take photos of birds too.

- a PDA with special bird-recording software.

Habitats

Different birds live in different places, called habitats. The next eight pages will help you enjoy birds in a range of habitats.

Gardens and parks

Your garden or a local park is a great place to start birding. You can watch birds often and get to know some common species well.

● Make your garden attractive to birds. Provide food, water and nesting places (see pages 36–37).

● Learn the differences between Blue and Great Tits, Song Thrushes and Blackbirds, Dunnocks and House Sparrows, Collared Doves and Woodpigeons.

Robin and Blackbird. Easy to see and interesting.

● Watch bird behaviour. Which birds drive others away? Where do different species feed?

● House Sparrows, Starlings, Swifts, House Martins and Jackdaws nest in chimneys, roofs and gutters. Robins sometimes nest in sheds!

● In the summer, watch the sky for Swifts, Swallows and House Martins.

● Visit parks when there are not too many people around. Make sure a grown-up knows what you're doing.

● Play areas with swings and slides aren't good for birds. Parks with grassy areas, trees, bushes and water are better.

Other garden and park birds to look for: Great Spotted Woodpecker, Song Thrush, Redwing, Fieldfare, Blackcap, Coal Tit, Long-tailed Tit, Siskin, Greenfinch, Chaffinch, Goldfinch, Magpie.

Above: Blue Tit.
Left: Robin, Blackbird, House Sparrow.

22

Most of the UK is farmland. Some farms have animals, like cows, sheep or pigs, others just grow cereals, vegetables or fruit. Many wild birds live on farmland too, with different birds on different types of farms.

Goldfinches. The yellow wing-bars are obvious.

● Watch hedges carefully for tits, finches, buntings thrushes and warblers. Bigger trees, and hedges with more than one type of tree or bush, are the best.

● In winter, check bare fields for flocks of birds such as gulls, Woodpigeons and Stock Doves, Lapwings and Golden Plovers, Rooks and Jackdaws, Starlings, Redwings and Fieldfares, finches, buntings, Skylarks.

● Lapwing, Redshank and Snipe breed in damp, grassy areas.

● Look up and listen for Skylarks – they sing from February until mid-summer in some places.

● If there's rough grassland, try an early morning or late evening visit – and hope for a Barn Owl.

Yellowhammer

Take care. Make sure you are allowed to be there and it is safe. Don't walk across farm fields unless there are public footpaths. Make sure a grown-up knows what you are doing.

Other farmland birds to look for: Buzzard, Little Owl, Turtle Dove, Swallow, Whitethroat, Bullfinch.

Left: Skylark
Far left: If you see Lapwings, look for Golden Plovers too. There aren't any here though!

Woodland

Wherever you live, there is probably woodland nearby. Even small patches are worth exploring. Woodlands are made up of deciduous trees (most of which have no leaves in the winter), coniferous trees (most of which have leaves all year round) or a mixture of both. Deciduous or mixed

A Willow Warbler's song will help you tell it from a Chiffchaff.

woodlands are normally best for birding. Woodland birds may be there, but they can be hard to see.

● Walk slowly and stop often. Use your eyes and ears. Learn the common woodland species' songs. The Chiffchaff's is easy to learn in early spring, but don't confuse it with the Great Tit's *tea-cher* song.

● Look for bird movement – from tree to tree, between leaves and twigs and on trunks and branches.

● Sit and watch. Sometimes you see more by waiting than by walking. A pool where birds drink is a good place to watch.

● Don't just look up. Look at ground level for thrushes, Wrens and Dunnocks and higher up for finches, tits, pigeons and warblers. Check trunks and branches for woodpeckers, Nuthatches, Treecreepers and sometimes, tits.

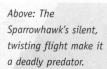

Above: The Sparrowhawk's silent, twisting flight make it a deadly predator.

Right: Dunnocks are handsome and have a sweet singing voice. But not everyone notices them.

● In spring and early summer migrants arrive and many birds sing. Go birding before the leaves come out and block your view! The beginning and end of the day are best.

- The wood's sheltered side (away from the wind) may have more birds in it. Look for sunny patches. Insects are more active there, and insects are good bird food!

- Glades and clearings are lighter, contain different plants and attract insects. They are another good feeding area for birds.

- Watch the edge of the wood from outside – you can see the whole height of the trees, which isn't easy from inside the wood.

- In winter look for mixed tit flocks – Blue Tits and Great Tits searching for food together. Sometimes other species join the flock – Goldcrests, a Treecreeper or other tit species. If you don't find the flock, you might think there are no birds in the wood! You may hear high-pitched squeaks and harsh chattering before you see the flock.

Nuthatch (top) and Wren (above). Two woodland birds with loud voices.

- Search coniferous woods for Coal Tit, Goldcrest, Mistle Thrush, and Siskin.

- Enjoy an upland oak wood in the summer, and look for Pied Flycatcher, Redstart and Wood Warbler.

Other woodland birds to look for: Sparrowhawk, Buzzard, Stock Dove, Tawny Owl, Blackcap, Garden Warbler, Willow Warbler, Spotted Flycatcher, Marsh Tit, Willow Tit.

Tawny Owl. Voles beware!

Lakeside bird watching can be wonderful. Birds feed over, on and under the water, and around muddy shores. They rest and nest on islands and vegetation. Trees and bushes nearby provide even more opportunities for birds.

Wigeon breed in Iceland, Scandinavia and Siberia. Thousands winter in the UK.

Grey Heron. One of our biggest birds.

● Scan the whole lake several times. Birds dive or hide behind islands and in vegetation – you won't see everything in one look.

● Common Terns, Canada Geese and Mute Swans nest on islands. In winter, look for roosting ducks and gulls, and Cormorants wing-drying.

● Check gull and duck flocks carefully. There may be more than one species in there!

● Kingfishers fly low and fast over the water. Look for an orange and blue blur. They perch in trees overhanging the water, or on posts sticking out of the water. Get used to their high-pitched whistle.

● Swifts, Swallows, House Martins and Sand Martins feed on insects over water. Hobbies may feed on these insect-eaters.

● Check the vegetation around the edges for Reed Warblers and Sedge Warblers (you'll probably hear them first), and also for Reed Buntings.

Other lake birds to look for: Great Crested Grebe, Little Grebe, Grey Heron, Wigeon, Teal, Gadwall, Shoveler, Tufted Duck, Pochard, Goldeneye, Little Ringed Plover, Green Sandpiper, Grey Wagtail.

Kingfisher. Stunning!

The UK coastline includes sandy beaches, pebbly beaches, rocky cliffs and islands. Some bits are wild; others are packed with holiday-makers. There are always birds to look for.

Gulls often gather in large flocks. Most of these are Black-headed Gulls. Can you see any that aren't?

● Enjoy Puffins, Guillemots, Razorbills, Kittiwakes and Gannets at a noisy, smelly seabird colony! In Ireland, and Scotland there are Black Guillemots too.

● If there are cliffs, there could be Fulmars, relatives of albatrosses. Peregrines and Kestrels nest on cliffs too.

● Look out to sea. There could be Cormorants, Shags, Eiders, Gulls, Terns and bright white Gannets. Don't look just once – birds fly past, dive, or disappear behind waves.

● Gulls come close. Have a good look at them. It takes four years for Herring Gulls to become adults. Use a field guide to work out how old they are.

● Little Terns and Ringed Plovers nest on shingle beaches. There may be fences to protect them. Take care not to disturb them.

● Rock Pipits like rocky areas, and Sanderlings like sandy beaches.

● Turnstones, Starlings, Rock Pipits, Carrion Crows and Hooded Crows like feeding along high tide lines.

Other coastal birds to look for: Eider, Purple Sandpiper, Sandwich Tern, Stonechat, Raven, Jackdaw.

Gannets nest close together at a gannetry.

Puffins

Estuaries

Estuaries are where rivers join the sea. When the tide goes out, mud is uncovered. It's stuffed with invertebrates, excellent food for waders and wildfowl, especially in the winter and during migration.

Dunlins in winter plumage. They have lost the black belly of their breeding plumage.

● Check the tide times in local papers, the internet, *The Birdwatchers' Yearbook* or birding magazines. Visit just before high tide for the best views.

● Keep the sun behind you or it may be difficult to see colours clearly.

● Scan more than once. Birds move, dive and hide.

● Learn the most common waders – Oystercatcher, Ringed Plover, Lapwing, Knot, Turnstone, Dunlin, Redshank and Curlew. Then it's easier to spot something unusual.

Shelduck

● When a flock suddenly takes off, look for a hunting Peregrine.

● Look at the water too. There could be grebes, ducks, geese, swans, gulls and Cormorants.

● If there are hides, use them! They can give great, close views and are warmer.

Curlew

Be careful: don't walk out on the mud. It can be very soft and the tide can come in quickly. Estuaries can be cold, so dress to stay warm and dry.

Other estuary birds to look for: Great Crested Grebe, Grey Heron, Shelduck, Wigeon, Pintail, Rock Pipit.

Grey Plovers – big and chunky. And a Dunlin.

Buzzard

Most of our 'uplands' (hills and mountains) are in the north and west. There aren't many kinds of upland birds, but some of them are hard to see anywhere else.

- Walk a little, stop and scan. Look for movement and birds perched on boulders or fences. Watch the sky.

- This is grouse country. Red Grouse are the easiest to see.

- Meadow Pipits are common. Their *see-see-see* call and song flights give them away. Don't confuse them with Skylarks.

- A small bird with a white rump flying away is probably a Wheatear.

Red Grouse – with wonderful red 'eyebrows'.

- Look for Stonechats and Whinchats. Stonechats are easier to see; Whinchats prefer damper areas.

- Predators include Merlins, Hen Harriers, Peregrines, and, in Scotland, Golden Eagles. Short-eared Owls breed on some moors. This owl flies in daylight!

- Watch out for Ravens – don't mistake them for birds of prey, Carrion Crows or Hooded Crows.

- Some waders breed here. They look fantastic, especially Dunlin and Golden Plover. Look for Curlew, Snipe, Redshank and Lapwing, too.

Don't go to the uplands on your own! Take an adult with you – they can be dangerous places and it is easy to get lost.

Other upland birds to look for: Black Grouse, Cuckoo, Twite, Ring Ouzel.

From left to right: Whinchat, Golden Eagle, Stonechat and Ring Ouzel.

Where to go

You don't need to travel far to see birds. Wherever you live, there will be some nearby. Start by spending time getting to know your local birds. The better you know the common species, the easier it will be to identify something unusual. Your garden or a local park is a good starting point.

A local patch

Once you're familiar with your immediate surroundings, find somewhere else nearby with more bird variety. Birders call this a 'local patch'. Watching a local patch is a great thing to do. It's easy, because it's close, and you learn a lot by watching the same area regularly. There may be no other people looking at birds there, so any information you collect could be useful for conservation too (see page 40).

When you are going birding, always make sure that a grown-up knows where you are going and what you will be doing.

A good local patch:

● has a variety of habitats – so there's a bigger variety of birds

● has open water, such as a pond or river – but don't worry if you can't find anywhere with water

● is easy to get to – you can walk or cycle there quickly

● needs no more than an hour and a half for a visit

● is a safe place to go.

REAL LOCAL PATCHES

You can see on the map that Areas A and B are close together. They are different parts of the same local patch. In Area A (top) Green Woodpeckers and Fieldfares feed in the paddocks and Yellowhammers use the hedges. Area B (middle) is a scrubby area good for seeing Whitethroat, Linnet and Willow Warbler.

Area C (bottom) is a different local patch, with open water and strips of woodland around the edges. Great Crested Grebes breed here and Common Sandpipers visit during migration.

Using a map

To find a local patch talk to local people you know, or use an Ordnance Survey (OS) map. You might be surprised at what's nearby, even if you think you know your area well. Maps come in different scales. If you can find one, use a 1:25,000-scale map. This has more detail than a 1:50,000 map. If there are no maps at home, a library may have some. Alternatively visit the OS website – www.ordnancesurvey.co.uk/oswebsite/getamap – you can look at small areas of maps online and print them.

Use the key on the map to find out if there is water or woodland, both of which are good in a local patch. Or choose an area with trees and rough grassland, or an old churchyard. There are no rules; just find somewhere with a bit of variety. The map will help you work out where you are allowed to walk. Look for 'public rights of way' and 'other public access' on the key.

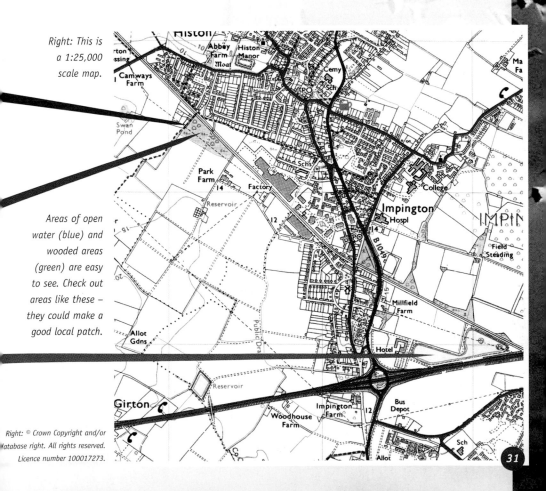

Right: This is a 1:25,000 scale map.

Areas of open water (blue) and wooded areas (green) are easy to see. Check out areas like these – they could make a good local patch.

Keep visiting

Get to know your local patch well. Go there often, at different times of day and different times of year. After a while, you will get to know its birds very well – probably better than anyone else.

Try to work out:

- which birds live where

- whether a bird is there all year round (a resident species) or just for part of the year (a migrant species)

- what the different species sound like

- which species look different from winter to summer, and when their appearance changes

- whether birds are doing different things at different times of year.

Once you're hooked, you will want to go to other good bird places, too.

Further from home

Travelling a short distance could bring even more birds within your reach. But to do this, you need to know where to go, and be able to get there. Here are some ideas to help you find the best birding places to visit:

- ask any local birders you know

- look in your county bird report at your local library or at your local bird club.

- look in a site guide ("Where to Watch Birds" books). These cover different parts of the UK and Ireland

Turtle Dove

Spotted Flycatcher

- look in the *Birdwatcher's Yearbook* (see page 55)

- get on the web. If your local bird club has a website, that might help. Some national birding websites are useful, too (see pages 52 and 55).

You might be able to cycle or use public transport to get to some of the sites safely. This isn't always possible, so you may have to persuade someone to take you, or find out if there is a local RSPB Wildlife Explorers group (see page 54). If there is, they may organise trips to good bird sites.

Lesser Spotted Woodpecker

Family days out - visiting nature reserves

You may live near a nature reserve. If you don't, finding a way to visit one is a challenge you could set yourself. There are more than you may think, and many are near towns. Check the map inside the front cover and then visit the RSPB's website to find out more about its nature reserves. Check out the Wildfowl and Wetlands Trust and your local Wildlife Trust websites, too.

Remember: to see a variety of birds, you need to visit a variety of habitats. Pages 22–29 describe birds and bird watching in some different habitats. Don't forget to tell a grown-up where you are going. They might want to come with you – if they do, make sure they see some birds too!

Three ways to find some good bird watching sites.

Birding action

Once you've got your binoculars and found a good place to look for birds, what next? How can you improve your chances? Experienced bird watchers make it look easy. This section tells you how.

Getting closer to birds

You don't need to dress like a commando in full camouflage gear! Dull-coloured clothes are generally better than bright colours, but it's more important that what you wear protects you from the weather. This might mean gloves, a hat (that doesn't cover your ears, or you won't hear birds very well) and lots of layers in winter, or a sunhat and suncream in summer. Wellington boots are good if you're going to wet or muddy places. Try to wear clothes that don't rustle too much – it will be easier to hear birds.

When to go

You can see or hear birds at almost any time of day, but some times are better than others. The worst time is normally the middle of the day, especially during really hot weather. One hour after dawn is the most active time for birds, but late afternoon and early evening are good times too. Waders and other birds that feed when the tide goes out are different. They will feed in the middle of the night if the tide is right!

The right approach

How you move is more important than what you wear. Move slowly and gently, looking carefully for signs of bird movement. Stop and look around frequently. With practice you will see the difference between a twig moving in the wind and a warbler moving in a treetop. Look up and behind you, too. Use your ears – you will hear many birds before you see them. Some you may hear but never see – such as Cuckoos or Tawny Owls.

Move carefully and use cover to get closer to birds.

TOP TIP

Use your binoculars to **search** for birds. Don't use them just to look at birds you have already found with your naked eyes. Habitat edges – where one habitat meets another – are good places to look. Pages 22–29 give you some more ideas.

A good viewpoint

When you can, keep the sun behind you or to one side. It's difficult to see birds well if you're looking into the sun. Keeping trees, bushes, hedges or a slight rise in the land between you and the birds makes it easier to get closer. You can stalk birds by getting down low, or even lying on your belly. This can be an exciting way of getting some good, close views. Try not to stand on the skyline – your shape will be very obvious and nervous birds will fly away.

Hides are for everyone. Don't miss out.

Using hides

Hides can give you great views, and are more comfortable and warmer than being completely outside.

When you are in a hide:

- talk quietly

- don't stick your arms out of the windows – this might frighten off any nearby birds

- listen to what other people say they are seeing, then make up your own mind – they might be wrong!

- scan the whole area in front of the hide for birds – don't wait for other people to point them out. Look near to the hide and far away. Look in all directions and watch the sky, too.

Immature Starling

You can't always get out and about, or travel, to watch birds. But there are ways you can attract them to your area. If you have a garden, try making it better for birds. There are many things you can do to create your own mini nature reserve.

Feeding

You can make bird feeders or buy them. If you buy one, buy a good one – cheap feeders don't always work that well and don't last any longer than home-made ones. Put the feeders where you can see them easily from the house. To protect feeding birds, don't put feeders too low or anywhere near where cats could hide. Clean the feeders from time to time. Do this outside and wash your hands afterwards. Dirty feeders can spread diseases to visiting birds. Most people use sunflower seeds or special seed mixes in their feeders. Try to buy bird food from a specialist bird food supplier if you can (see page 55).

Greenfinches love sunflower seed. Goldfinches like it too.

Alternatively, you can feed the birds scraps from your home.

Here are some ideas to get you started:

apples; small pieces of bacon rind; cheese; boiled or baked potato; raw pastry; bread; biscuit crumbs; nuts (not salted); and oats (not cooked).

Great Tit, Nuthatch, Robin and Great Spotted Woodpecker. An excellent feeding station.

Water

Birds need water for drinking and bathing. A flower pot tray about 30cm across is good for this. Put out water regularly and keep it clean and topped up. A pond is even better and will attract lots of other wildlife too. Make sure it's got some shallow edges.

Right: This Woodpigeon is drinking at a pond, but even small areas of water can attract birds.

Left: An immature Blue Tit checks out the outside world.

Nest sites

Put up nestboxes in your garden. Different designs suit different species – some have holes, others have open fronts. You can buy them or make them. Put nestboxes somewhere safe from cats, ideally where you can watch them from a safe distance. Face them north or east to avoid overheating the chicks inside in the summer. Blue Tits and Great Tits often nest in nestboxes. Starlings and House Sparrows are getting rarer, so you could put up boxes for these too. Nestboxes can be put up at any time of year, but it's best to get them up by the end of January ready for birds to use in spring – if you're lucky!

Gardening

Talk to whoever looks after your garden, or get involved yourself. Investigate plants that are good for wildlife. You will need to find out which species might grow in your garden. Try to grow plants that provide seeds or fruit for birds to eat, plants that attract insects, and plants that provide shelter and nesting places.

TOP TIP

Take a small bag of bird seed with you when you go birding. If you plan to end up where you started, scatter some seed on the ground near the beginning of your walk. When you get back there, have a look to see if any birds are feeding on it. Ask permission before you do this on a nature reserve, farm or country park.

Now you've got close to birds, here are some other tips you might find useful.

Pointing out a bird

If you want to show a bird to someone else, you may need to help them find it. Try:

● giving directions from things that are easy to see ("it's below the big tree"; "just to the right of the black and white cow"; "right next to the signpost")

● using the clock method ('it's about 50 metres away at 11 o'clock". See below.)

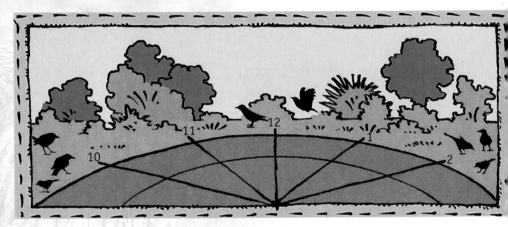

If you are seawatching (watching birds on or flying over the sea), describing a bird's position can be even harder, especially if it keeps disappearing behind waves. The clock method helps, or you could use these questions to help describe the bird's position:

Go seawatching and you might see a Manx Shearwater. The shearwater on the right is at 2 o'clock.

- Is the bird flying to the left or the right?

- Is it above or below the horizon?

- How far out is it – halfway out?

- Are there any boats or buoys you can use to help? ("It's flying left, just past the orange buoy.")

Putting birds first

Make sure your bird watching doesn't harm any birds, or upset farmers or other landowners. Remember:

- Birds always come first! Do nothing that might harm them. Disturb them as little as possible.

- Protect habitats. Take care when you are bird watching not to damage the places birds live.

- Don't bird watch on private property unless you know you are allowed to be there.

- Be polite and considerate to other people you meet when you are bird watching.

- Send your bird records to your local bird recorder (see page 41) and put them on BirdTrack (www.birdtrack.net) too.

- Follow the bird protection laws. Contact the RSPB (see page 54) for a free copy of *Birds and the Law*.

Making it count

Your birding can produce information that's useful for conservation – especially if you are the only person watching your local birds. A notebook, or some other form of on-the-spot record, is essential for collecting accurate information. You won't be able to remember everything if you wait until you get home.

Try to note down:

- the birds you saw
- when and where you saw them
- how many you saw
- any interesting behaviour or other observations
- the weather conditions.

Here's an example:

Wind coming from the south

This means about ten

2 swans were seen. Then another 2 with 7 young swans

About fifteen males and 5 females

Mute Swan

Great Crested Grebe

Green Woodpecker

Lesser Black-backed Gull.

Long-Tailed Tit

Not just birds! A butterfly too.

Ad. means adult.
Juv. means juvenile.

Probably 1, flying to the west

3 June 05 Dudburgh Lake
9.35am – 11.15am
Warm + Bright. Wind S light

Chiffchaff c10
M.Swan 2\2 ⑦
Mallard c20 c15 ♂♂
GCG 2 ①
Greenwood 2 Ad.with
LBBG 1prob→w juv.on back
Blackcap 1 ♂\♂\1♀
Lt.Tit
Speckled Wood

To make your information count, you need to send it to the local bird recorder. You

can find out who this is by looking in the *Birdwatcher's Yearbook* (see page 55) or on one of the birding websites (Fat Birder, for example). Local bird recorders will be particularly interested in anything you see that proves a bird is breeding, or trying to breed. This includes birds singing in the breeding season, birds carrying nesting material, and young birds that have recently left the nest.

Numbers matter

Bird recorders will also be interested in unusually large counts of any species. 'Large' means different things for different species. A flock of 12 Bullfinches might not be difficult to count, but it is a rare enough sight to make it worth telling the recorder.

Some species form much bigger flocks containing hundreds or thousands of birds. These are hard to count – the flock might be flying, or some of the birds might be hidden. You won't get a completely accurate count of a big flock. The aim is to make a good estimate. To do this, count part of the flock – 30 birds, for example. If the flock looks roughly four times bigger than the section you counted, your estimate is 120 birds. If it's roughly seven times bigger, estimate 210 birds. There's another example in the photo below.

20 birds counted. This is about a quarter of the flock so your estimate is 20 x 4 = 80 birds. These are Black-tailed Godwits.

Above and right: Don't forget common birds like House Sparrows and Blackbirds. Make a note of your counts of these species too.

Ordinary is interesting

Routine records can be important, too. Recorders are sometimes short of records of common birds, because no one bothers to tell them. There are far fewer House Sparrows and Starlings than there used to be. Data about common birds can help conservationists spot changes in populations – hopefully, before it's too late.

Declare if it's rare

Local recorders will also be interested in any rare birds you see. They will have to be sure that you really did see what you think you saw – they will want to see the notes you made to identify the bird. Part of their job is to make sure that any birds that are recorded are accurately identified.

You can send in your records to local recorders by post, or sometimes by e-mail. Some people send them in once a year, others more often. If you see a rare bird, send in the details as soon as possible. Once a year, a county bird report is published. If you have sent in records, you will probably find your name in it.

ToP TIP

Find out who your local bird recorder is and send in your records. Your observations will be added to a database and may help conserve birds in the future.

You can also make a difference by collecting data

for a survey organised by the British Trust for Ornithology (BTO), the RSPB or another conservation body. Here are some things you could try.

Big Garden Birdwatch/Big Schools' Birdwatch

This takes place during the last weekend of January and has been running since 1979. Hundreds of thousands of people take part and it only takes an hour. You can find out more at www.rspb.org.uk, or in RSPB or RSPB Wildlife Explorer magazines.

Birdtrack

A great way to put your bird watching records to good use. It's organised by the BTO, and is all online. You can find out more at www.birdtrack.net

BTO surveys

The BTO organises a range of surveys. Check out www.bto.org for more information.

Nature's calendar

Record information about a range of natural events to observe how climate change is affecting birds. See www.phenology.org.uk

Left: Little Egrets are getting commoner, perhaps because of climate change.

Right: A Barn Owl. Definitely worth telling the bird recorder about!

WARNING

Data can often be submitted online, but you may have to register on some websites. Check with your parents or guardians before you do this.

The birder's year

Here are some suggestions for birding activities throughout the year. You'll need an adult's help for some of them, so use these pages to persuade someone to lend a hand!

January

● Start a year list – a tally of all the bird species you see during the year.

● Listen out for the few birds that sing in winter. Learn their songs before spring when the air is full of bird song and it's much more confusing. Try to learn the songs of the Robin, Song Thrush, Mistle Thrush, Great Tit and Dunnock (see page 9 to find out how).

*Robin. One of the species to look for in **Big Garden Birdwatch**.*

● Get ready for the **Big Garden Birdwatch** (see page 43) which takes place during the last weekend of January. Feed the birds in your garden and send in your results online if you can. Or, ask your teacher if your class could do **Big Schools' Birdwatch**.

● Look for local feeding flocks of buntings (Yellowhammer, Reed Bunting and sometimes other species), finches and larks (from November to March).

The breeding season has already begun for Rooks (below) and Mistle Thrushes (bottom).

February

● Blackbirds start singing. Learn their song and add it to the list of bird songs you recognise (see page 9).

● If you are putting up nestboxes, get them up by the middle of the month at the latest.

● Watch some early nest-building activity at your nearest rookery (where lots of rooks nest in one place) or heronry (where lots of herons nest together). Mistle Thrushes and Blackbirds build nests early, too.

● Visit an estuary to see wintering waders and wildfowl. If the coast is too far away, visit an inland wetland to see wintering ducks, geese and swans (November to February).

Signs of spring. Wheatears (above) arrive in March, House Martins (left), in April.

• This is the month when summer migrants really begin to arrive. Start a list of the dates on which you first see each migrant species. Wheatear, Little Ringed Plover, Sand Martin, Chiffchaff and Sandwich Tern are among the first. Look out for organisations collecting summer migrant dates, and send them your information. The further north you are, the later the birds will get to you. Watch the sky, too – you might see migrants flying over.

• Watch your local birds for signs of nesting. They may be carrying nesting material or, later in the month, taking food to the nest. House Sparrows, Starlings, Blackbirds and Collared Doves are good ones to watch. You could help out by putting out pet fur, straw and other materials for them to collect.

• Spend time in your local woodland. Use this period before the leaves come out to identify some of the different birds that are singing. Try to learn the songs of the Chaffinch, Willow Warbler, Wren, Dunnock and Blackcap (see page 9).

• Keep watching for migrants arriving.

• Visit a nature reserve that includes several different habitats, ideally on the coast. Look out for summer visitors, birds passing through on migration and lots of breeding activity (from April to May).

• Check out the RSPB's website (see page 55) to discover which **Aren't Birds Brilliant!** sites are open. If you can get to one you could see Ospreys, Peregrines, Puffins or other brilliant species.

Right: Like many birds in April, this Puffin is busy nest building.

● This is baby bird month. Watch your local birds to see how many young the different species have, and what they are eating. The young birds will look different from their parents – more to learn! If you find a baby bird, don't pick it up! Get a *Baby Birds* leaflet from the RSPB. It tells you exactly what to do.

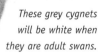

Great Crested Grebe chicks are stripy and hitch rides on a parent's back.

● Listen to the dawn chorus. Persuade someone to take you to a wood, country park or nature reserve, or just get up early (about 4.00am!), open the window and listen. Do it just before daylight for the best experience – it's early, but worth it!

● Watch out for the last of the summer migrants arriving.

● Visit a heathland at dusk to look and listen for Nightjars and Woodcock. Or try a wetland for Snipe, Reed Warblers, Sedge Warblers, Grasshopper Warblers and more (May to June).

These grey cygnets will be white when they are adult swans.

June

● The breeding season continues – keep an eye on what your local birds are up to.

● Visit a seabird colony – be prepared for lots of birds, noise and smells! You could see Puffins, Guillemots, Razorbills, Kittiwakes, Fulmars and Gannets (from June to July).

● If you get the chance, try birding on moorland or mountains. You could see Red Grouse, Golden Plover and Curlew (from May to July).

Gannets. Spectacular!

- Some waders are already migrating south. Visit a wetland to look for them – Spotted Redshank, Grey Plover, Green Sandpiper and Curlew Sandpiper are all possible (from July to August).

- Watch for young birds locally. Juveniles may look different to adults – get to know them.

Above: Green Sandpiper. On its way south from its breeding grounds.

- If you're at the coast, look out to sea. You could see migrating seabirds, including skuas and shearwaters. The east, south and south-west coasts are good locations at this time of year.

- Take a birding boat trip for great encounters with skuas, shearwaters, auks and more. There are a few places where boats go to sea, just to look for birds. Some of the best go from Bridlington in Humberside.

Left: Get close to seabirds.
Far left: Manx Shearwater: a long-lived, long distance traveller.

- Clean your birdfeeders, fill them up and put them out in your garden. Remember, you can feed birds all year round if you want to.

- Watch out for late Swifts, young Chiffchaffs moving through gardens, and other summer visitors that are starting to head south this month. Look up and you might see flocks of migrating Swallows and House Martins.

Time to fill up the feeders.

October

- If you have nestboxes, clean them out. They'll be ready for next spring, and some birds might use them to roost in over winter (October to November).

Dungeness. An RSPB nature reserve on the Kent coast.

- Migrants are moving. An October day at a nature reserve on the coast can be fantastic, but get there early.

- Look for Redwings and Fieldfares in your garden, local fields or hedges. These thrushes breed in Scandinavia and spend winter in the UK.

Wintering geese arrive in October. You could see Brent Geese or Pink-footed Geese at the coast.

November

- Find out where your nearest Starling roost is and take an early evening look. It could be spectacular.

- Many trees are leafless – use your binoculars to look among the branches for nests that were used earlier in the year.

- Waxwings may begin to arrive – especially in the east. If you hear of any near you, go to see them – they are well worth it. Or, you might be lucky and find your own first.

A Starling roost. A lot of birds!

December

- Visit a gull roost towards the end of the afternoon. The big flocks are impressive – and you can practise your gull identification (September to March).

Gulls. Ideal for testing your skills on a cold winter's day!

Use these suggestions to get the most out of your school holidays. Here are things you can do at home, and away from home.

Easter

Look out for:

- signs of breeding
- summer migrants.

Check out:

- a nature reserve with lots of different habitats. One on the coast is best. Visit as late in April as possible – more migrants will be in

- an **Aren't Birds Brilliant!** site. Check the RSPB website (www.rspb.org.uk) for details of when each site opens

- the dawn chorus.

Why not:

- learn how to make your own bird food? Look at the RSPB website for tips.

Summer

Look out for:

- juvenile birds

- butterflies and dragonflies – definitely worth a look!

Check out:

- a coastal wetland

- seawatching

- a birding boat trip

- a seabird colony

- an **Aren't Birds Brilliant!** site.

Why not:

- keep a list of all the birds you see during the holiday?

Christmas

Look out for:

- winter thrushes

- finch, bunting and lark flocks

- feeding flocks in local woodland.

Check out:

- an estuary

- a wildfowl spectacle.

Why not:

- make a nestbox and put it up before the breeding season starts.

Right: Help homeless birds.
Build a nestbox.

49

On your travels

Holidays are a great chance to look for birds in new places. If you are the only birder in your family, take these tips to get some birds into your holiday.

Holidays at home

The UK has lots of holiday destinations with interesting birds nearby. Weymouth in Dorset has an RSPB reserve right next to the railway station. There are excellent views of the Exe estuary from hides at Dawlish Warren in Devon, a nature reserve close to the holidaymakers' beach. In Lancashire, Southport Pier is great for seeing estuary birds, and there are Ospreys in the Lake District as well as Scotland.

Norfolk. Good for family holidays, and birds.

All the fun of the fair and birds too. Southport.

These are just a few examples. Do your research before you go – you might be surprised at the possibilities! Check the RSPB's website to see if there's an **Aren't birds brilliant!** site in the area you're visiting or the map inside the front cover for UK RSPB nature reserves.

Some places might interest the rest of the family while providing some birding too. The grounds around historic buildings and stately homes can be good for birds. Most people enjoy boat trips around islands – and these can be great for seeing many kinds of wildlife.

Be prepared

Keep your binoculars with you at all times. You might be surprised. Take care on the beach, though – sand in binoculars is not a good idea, as it can scratch the lenses.

> **TOP TIP**
>
> *Try persuading your family that everyone can choose an activity for one or two days of the holiday. Your choice can be a visit to the best birding place in the area!*

Holidays abroad can provide exciting introductions to bird species that you have never seen before. There are exciting birds almost everywhere. For example, a holiday in the south of Spain could include Bee-eaters, vultures and even flamingoes.

All the tips in this book will work abroad, though the research will be harder. There are site guides ("Where to Watch Birds" books) for many parts of the world. Try these, or see what you can find out on the web. Make sure you have a good field guide for the area too.

Any holiday can include birds. If you stay in a hotel, there may be birds around the hotel's grounds. If you are staying at a busy resort, you could try a walk just outside the resort.

Once you get away from the crowds, there will probably be birds. Don't forget to watch the sea. The Mediterranean Sea, for example, can be a good place to see shearwaters.

Enjoy your holiday!

There are some fantastic birds around the Mediterranean. You could see stripy, crested Hoopoes (above top) and colourful Bee-eaters (left). The best bit of a holiday in Florida might be diving Brown Pelicans (above centre)!

51

Taking it further

If you've read this far, this book won't be enough! There are many things you can do to take your interest further. Here are some ideas:

Join up

RSPB Wildlife Explorers is the junior membership of the RSPB. Join and take part in competitions, events, projects and even holidays. There are local groups where you can meet other young people who are into birds and wildlife. And you get six magazines a year too. Find out more at: www.rspb.org.uk/youth

Making birdcake. Wildlife Explorer groups don't just watch birds.

Get a magazine

Bird Watching magazine is good to start with. It comes out once a month and is full of articles about birds and birding. For something more advanced, try *Birdwatch*.

Explore the web

There are lots of bird watching websites. Try the ones on the right first, or see if your local bird club has one. Always make sure a grown-up knows what you're doing when you're online.

WEBSITES TO VISIT

RSPB youth pages
www.rspb.org.uk/youth

UK bird watching links
www.birdlinks.co.uk

Fat Birder
www.fatbirder.com

Get a telescope

For really great views of birds, far away or close up, invest in a telescope. You will also need a good tripod to put it on. A magnification of 20–30x is plenty for most situations. The views can be good, but it can be awkward carrying the equipment.

Do your research before you buy. Watch the birding magazines for reviews. Buy from a specialist shop and hunt for second-hand bargains. A good telescope doesn't have to be too expensive.

Make it big! Try to look through a friend's telescope if you don't have your own.

Start digiscoping

Put a digital camera over the eyepiece of a telescope and you can take great pictures of birds. Many 'digiscopers' use special adaptors to hold the camera in the right position over the eyepiece. It will take practice to get good pictures, but any pictures you take might help you identify a bird later. Some digiscopers put their pictures on the web. This means that other people can see the bird on their computer very soon after the bird was sighted for real.

Become a ringer

Ringers catch birds and put lightweight rings on their legs to find out more about bird movements and how long birds live. Seeing a bird in the hand is an amazing experience. The BTO organises bird ringing in the UK and they want more young ringers. It takes years of training to learn the skills to become fully licensed, so you will need to be very keen and committed. To find out more, contact the BTO (see page 54).

Find out more about ringing at www.bto.org/ringing

Useful information

Organisations

RSPB Wildlife Explorers
The Lodge
Sandy
Beds SG19 2DL
Tel: 01767 680551
www.rspb.org.uk/youth

British Trust for Ornithology (BTO)
The National Centre for Ornithology
The Nunnery
Thetford
Norfolk IP24 2PU
Tel: 01842 750050
www.bto.org

Wildfowl and Wetlands Trust
Slimbridge
Gloucestershire GL2 7BT
Tel: 01453 891900
www.wwt.org.uk

The Wildlife Trusts (and Wildlife Watch)
The Kiln
Waterside
Mather Road
Newark
Nottinghamshire NG24 1WT
Tel: 0870 0367711
www.wildlifetrusts.org

Books

The BTO Nestbox Guide
By Chris Du Feu and Derek Toomer
BTO, 2003

RSPB Pocket Birdfeeder Guide
By Robert Burton
Dorling Kindersley, 2004

Robin

Kingfisher

54

The Bird-friendly Garden
By Stephen Moss
Harper Collins, 2004

The Birdwatcher's Yearbook
Buckingham Press
55 Thorpe Park Road
Peterborough PE3 6LJ
Tel: 01733 561739

Skylark

Great Tit

Multimedia

WildSounds: www.wildsounds.co.uk

Birdguides: www.birdguides.com

Other websites

BirdLife International: www.birdlife.org

Bird Links to the World:
www.bsc- eoc.org/links

Fat Birder: www.fatbirder.com

RSPB: www.rspb.org.uk

Surfbirds: www.surfbirds.com

UK bird watching links: www.birdlinks.co.uk

Disabled Birders' Association
www.disabledbirdersassociation.co.uk

Bird food and feeding suppliers

RSPB Sales Ltd: www.rspbshop.co.uk

CJ WildBird foods: www.birdfood.co.uk

The field guide

This short field guide (pages 56–125) will help you to identify most birds that you might see in the UK and Ireland. Look at the pictures and read the descriptions carefully. Make a note of where and when you saw the bird, and what it was doing. It is often best to start by ruling out what the bird is not.

Pictures

The pictures show each bird's shape, colour and markings, and the way it perches or flies. They also show any important differences between male and female or between breeding and non-breeding plumage. Beware: birds don't always look like their picture! A pale bird looks dark with the sun behind it. A slim bird can look fat in cold weather.

Descriptions

The first piece of information about each bird is its name and length. Be careful: these can sometimes be misleading. For instance, a Common Gull is not as 'common' as some other gulls. A Magpie's long tail makes it the same length as a Carrion Crow, even though it is really a smaller bird (see page 6).

Simple icons help you to find the key information about each bird and to make quick comparisons between different species. The box below explains what each one means.

IDENTIFICATION		This tells you what the bird looks like: its size, shape, colours and markings. 'Summer' refers to breeding plumage (roughly March to July, for most birds); 'winter' refers to non-breeding plumage (the rest of the year).
BEHAVIOUR		This tells you what the bird does – how it moves and feeds, whether it lives alone or in groups and any unusual habits it has.
VOICE		This tells you what noises the bird makes, including its songs and calls.
WHERE TO SEE		This tells you roughly where the bird lives and what kind of habitat it prefers. It also tells you when you are likely to see each species, and how common it is.
DON'T CONFUSE WITH		This lists other birds that look like the bird being described. Some might be from a different family (for instance, Swifts look a bit like Swallows, but are not related to them). Not all of them appear in this book, so you may have to look at other field guides too.

 : male   : female   : immature (non-adult plumage)

Little Grebe (25–29cm)

This is the smallest bird that swims on fresh water.

summer

winter

small size; dumpy shape with **fluffy rear end**; brown all over; reddish neck and cheeks in summer; paler in winter; bare patches at base of bill

dives often (and often re-surfaces out of sight); rivals chase each other over water, half running/half flying; young often ride on parents' backs; gathers in small groups during winter

loud, high-pitched trill

common, but can be hard to see; breeds on ponds, canals and slow-flowing rivers; moves to larger lakes in winter

Slavonian Grebe, Black-necked Grebe, young Moorhen or Coot

Great Crested Grebe (46–51cm)

This large, slim grebe sports fancy summer headgear.

slightly smaller than Mallard, with long neck and pointed bill; white underneath and brown above; in summer, **shaggy ruff on cheeks**; in winter, white and grey; white wing markings in flight

winter

dives often; rests head on back; rarely flies; pairs perform dancing courtship displays in spring; gathers in small groups during winter

mostly silent

common, except for northern Scotland; breeds on inland waters – often in towns; in winter, moves to larger lakes, reservoirs and sea

Red-necked Grebe, Goosander, Red-breasted Merganser, young Cormorant or Shag

summer

Fulmar (45–50cm)

This seabird's stiff-winged flight shows that it is not a gull.

- similar to medium-sized gull, but with shorter neck, stubbier bill and **straighter, narrower wings**; white, with mottled grey wings and dark eye

- glides smoothly along cliffs or low over water, with short bursts of flapping; nests in small colonies on cliffs; sometimes perches on sea

- cackling at nest

- breeds on cliffs all round coast; hardly ever seen inland; travels far out to sea.

- medium-sized gulls, Manx Shearwater

SECRET WEAPON

The Fulmar produces special oil in its stomach to feed its chicks. It can squirt this oil at any intruder that gets too close to the nest. The oil makes such a sticky, stinky mess that the intruder quickly backs off.

Gannet (87–100cm)

This huge, white seabird dives from high up to catch fish.

Diving for fish

- bigger than any gull, with long body, pointed wings and tail, and dagger-like bill; adult has **snow-white plumage, black wing tips and yellowish head**; young are grey-brown all over

- straight flight, with heavy flaps and long glides; when fishing, circles above sea and plunges in with a splash; flocks fish together; often sits on water

- cackling at nest

- breeds in big sea-cliff colonies in north and west; travels huge distances during winter and may be seen anywhere offshore

- large gulls, large shearwaters

Cormorant (80–100cm)

This large, dark water bird catches fish by diving from the surface.

long body and long, thick neck; powerful bill with hooked tip; **adult is black, with white patch on face and thigh in summer**; young are brown above and pale below

sits low in water with bill tilted upwards; dives with small leap; flies very straight, sometimes high up; likes to perch on sandbanks or jetties, often with wings outstretched

croaks and growls at nest

common in inland and coastal waters, including towns and cities; breeds in colonies on sea cliffs or trees beside lakes

Shag, divers, larger grebes, Goosander, Red-breasted Merganser

Shag (65–80cm)

Look closely: a 'Cormorant' on a rocky coast may be a Shag.

similar to Cormorant, but smaller, with thinner bill; blackish-green all over in summer, with small crest on forehead; young are brown, and paler below.

fishes just like Cormorant, but leaps forward more when diving; flies low over water; perches only on rocks – often with wings outstretched

grunting noises at nest

breeds on rocky coasts around north and west; nests low down on cliffs; likes rough water around rocks; seldom seen inland

Cormorant, divers, larger grebes, Goosander, Red-breasted Merganser

You can often see many other birds on the sea, especially during winter and migration times. Here are a few to look out for.

Long-tailed Duck
Black and white sea duck; male has long tail.

Common Scoter
All-dark sea duck; often in large flocks

Eider
Plump sea duck; breeding male is black and white

Great Skua
Big and dark; white wing patches; chases other birds

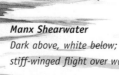

Red-breasted Merganser
Slim, long-billed sea duck; dives often

Red-throated Diver
Smallest, commonest diver; pale in winter

Manx Shearwater
Dark above, white below; stiff-winged flight over waves

A heron stands taller than any other water bird.

very tall, with long legs, long, thin neck and dagger-shaped bill; broad, rounded wings; mostly grey, with black and white markings; young are greyer all over

usually solitary; stands in shallow water with neck kinked, waiting to grab fish or frogs; rests hunched up; flies with slow wingbeats, neck drawn up and legs trailing

deep croak in flight

common on still inland waters and sheltered coasts; visits garden ponds for goldfish; breeds in large colonies in tall trees

Bittern, large gulls or large birds of prey (in flight)

This all-white heron often chases its prey through the shallows.

heron-shaped, but much smaller and **pure white all over**; black bill, black legs with yellow feet; rounded wings

usually solitary; always feeds in water; stands waiting for prey or chases it through shallow water with wings raised; flies with neck drawn up and legs trailing; roosts and breeds in trees beside water

usually silent, except at breeding colonies

southern parts of the UK on estuaries and marshes; gathers along coast in winter

gulls or Barn Owl (in flight)

Mute Swan (125–155cm)

This enormous, white waterfowl is Britain's largest bird.

- huge, with very long neck; adults are **all-white with orange-and-black bill**; young are dirty brown

- usually seen swimming in pairs or small groups; often holds folded wings raised; runs along surface to get airborne; wings make loud, whooshing sound in flight; can be aggressive

- hisses when angry

- common on inland waters, such as ponds, lakes and slow-flowing rivers; also in estuaries; the only Swan likely to be seen in towns

- Whooper and Bewick's Swan (winter only), white farmyard geese

FEATHER RECORD

Swans have more feathers on their body than any other bird. A Mute Swan has about 25,000 in total, of which over 80 per cent are on its head and neck.

Greylag Goose (75–90cm)

This common 'grey goose' is the ancestor of most domestic geese.

- large, fat goose, with long neck, orange bill and pink legs; greyish-brown plumage with white under tail; shows **pale grey forewing** and underwing in flight

- usually in flocks on or beside water; often grazes on farmland; flocks fly in straggly 'V' formations

- noisy cackling and honking – especially in flight

- widespread on inland waters, estuaries and marshes; 'true' wild Greylags breed only in northern Scotland, but feral birds are widespread; more common in winter.

- Pink-footed Goose, White-fronted Goose, Bean Goose

Pink-footed Goose: smaller and darker than Greylag, with small head, pink-and-black bill, pink legs and no grey on wings; flocks visit coastal marshes in winter.

Canada Goose (56–110cm)

This big, black-necked goose is a common sight in towns and parks.

taller and longer-necked than other geese, though varies greatly in size; brown body, with pale breast and white under tail; black head and neck with **white patch on cheeks**; black bill and legs

usually in flocks on water, or grazing on nearby grass; can upend to feed in deeper water; flocks fly in loose formation; often roosts on water

loud trumpeting

common, except for northern Scotland; prefers lowland inland waters – including reservoirs and city lakes

Brent Goose, Barnacle Goose

Brent Goose: smaller and darker than Canada Goose, with short bill and (in adults) white mark on side of black neck; winter visitor in large flocks to muddy estuaries.

Shelduck (58–67cm)

A big, mostly white duck on an estuary is probably a Shelduck.

larger than Mallard; **white, with greenish-black head and neck**, chestnut band around breast, and black wing markings; pink feet and red bill (knob on male's bill)

usually in pairs or family groups; swims and wades while feeding; sweeps bill through mud to sift small food; often nests in burrows

males are usually silent; female has low, growling call

all around coast, though less common in Scotland; prefers estuaries with mudflats and sandbanks; uncommon inland

male Shoveler, male Eider

♂

Wigeon (45–51cm)

You often see (and hear!) this duck in large flocks.

- slightly smaller than Mallard, with shorter neck and bill; male has grey body, **chestnut head, yellow forehead** and white stripe on side, with conspicuous white wing-patches in flight; female is brown, with white belly

- gathers in winter to graze on waterside grasses; also feeds in water; takes off in large flocks

- male has high-pitched whistle – *whee-ooo*; flocks often call together

- winter visitor to wetlands and coastal marshes; also lakes, reservoirs and gravel pits inland; small numbers breed in Scotland and northern England

- Teal, Mallard, Pochard.

Teal (34–38cm)

Don't miss this little duck feeding quietly by the water's edge.

- half the size of Mallard; male has chestnut head with dark green eye-patch, grey body with white stripe along flank and **yellow patch under tail**; female is brown and speckled, like small female Mallard

- feeds quietly in pairs or small groups; often upends; takes off vertically when alarmed and flies away very fast

- male makes short, high-pitched whistle

- widespread and common in winter; in summer, small numbers breed in quiet areas; prefers marshland and small patches of shallow water

- Mallard, Wigeon

Mallard (50–65cm)

This common duck is a familiar sight all over the world.

♀

♂

large duck with long bill; male is pale grey with **bottle-green head and white neck ring**, purplish breast, curly tail feathers and yellow bill; female is speckled brown with dark eye-stripe and orange bill; many domestic varieties

usually seen in pairs or small groups; often very tame; feeds by dipping head and neck underwater or upending

female makes typical duck quacking; male is quieter

on fresh water anywhere, from village ponds to coastal marshes; in winter sometimes also at sea

Gadwall, Teal, Wigeon

Gadwall (45–56cm)

This medium-sized duck is more common than many people realise.

similar shape to Mallard, but slightly smaller; male is **greyish-brown with black rear end**; female is like a slimmer, greyer female Mallard, with orange sides to bill; both sexes have white wing-patch which shows well in flight

feeds on the water's surface in pairs or small groups; often sits quietly at the water's edge

usually silent: female makes a high-pitched quack; male croaks in flight

most common in southern and eastern England; more widespread in winter; prefers large areas of water, including lakes and reservoirs

Mallard

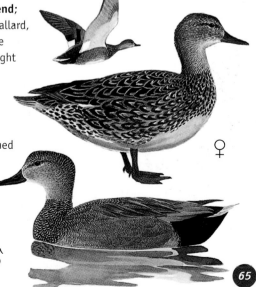

♀

♂

Shoveler (44–52cm)

Inside a Shoveler's long bill is a special sieve for filtering food.

- smaller than Mallard, with **long bill flattened like shovel**; male has greenish-black head and white underparts, with chestnut patch on flanks; female is speckled brown all over; in flight both show blue wing markings and have front-heavy shape

- usually seen feeding on water in pairs or small groups; bill touches surface when feeding; often sits quietly at water's edge

- mostly silent

- common and widespread, except northern Scotland; breeds on inland and coastal marshes; visits larger inland waters during winter

- Shelduck (male), Mallard (female)

Pintail (51–66cm)

No other freshwater duck has such a long pointed tail.

- Mallard-sized, but slimmer; male is mostly white-and-grey, with chocolate-brown head, **white stripe on neck and long, pointed black tail**; female is speckled brown like female Mallard, but with more pointed tail and no eye-stripe

- usually seen feeding on water, in pairs or small groups; often upends to reach food deep down with its long neck; flocks fly high in 'V' formation

- mostly silent

- a rare breeding bird, but widespread in winter on marshy and coastal areas

- Mallard (female)

Tufted Duck (40–47cm)

This black-and-white diving duck is common in built-up areas.

small diving duck; yellow eyes and blue-grey bill; male is glossy black with pure white flanks and **drooping crest**; female is dark brown with paler flanks and short crest; white wing-bars in flight

usually seen on the water; dives constantly for food; patters across surface to take off; can become tame in town parks

mostly silent

widespread and common on lakes, gravel pits and other inland waters; large flocks gather in winter

Goldeneye, Pochard (female), Scaup (female)

Goldeneye: black-and-white, like Tufted Duck, but with puffed-up-looking head; male has white breast and white patch on face; mostly winter visitor to inland waters and coasts

Pochard (42–49cm)

You can often see this dumpy diving duck alongside Tufted Ducks.

small, plump diving duck with rounded head and flat tail; male is **pale grey with reddish head and neck**, and black breast and tail; female is brown and grey; in flight, shows pale grey wing-bars.

dives for food from surface; regularly sleeps on water; runs to take off – like Tufted Duck

mostly silent

widespread on lakes, gravel pits and other inland waters; uncommon breeding bird, but common in winter when large flocks gather; often visits town parks

Tufted Duck (female), Goldeneye (female), Wigeon (male), Scaup (female)

Red Kite (60–66cm)

This big, angular bird of prey twists its forked tail in flight.

bigger than Buzzard, with longer wings and **long, forked tail**; reddish-brown body and reddish-orange tail; pale head and pale 'windows' in underwings

soars over open country looking for food; eats mostly dead animals; may gather in small groups to roost or feed

high-pitched *pee-ooo-eee*, similar to Buzzard

once nested only in Wales but now becoming more common in parts of England and Scotland; likes farmland with scattered woodland

Buzzard, harriers, Osprey

COMING HOME

Red Kites were confined to Wales for many years. But in 1989, scientists began to reintroduce them to places where they had lived centuries earlier. Now you can also see Red Kites in many parts of England and Scotland.

Buzzard (51–57cm)

You may hear a Buzzard's call before you spot it soaring high overhead.

big and stocky, with **broad, rounded wings**; brownish all over, but varies from dark to pale; wings show fingers and pale 'windows' underneath

soars high, with wings held in shallow 'V'; hunts small mammals such as rabbits; may hover, but looks clumsy compared to Kestrel; perches on fence posts and sometimes in fields

high-pitched, far-carrying *pee-uuuu*

widespread; most common in north and west; likes hilly country with scattered woodland; travels widely during winter

Red Kite, Golden Eagle, harriers, Rough-legged Buzzard, Honey Buzzard

Kestrel (32–35cm)

Except for quivering wings, a hovering kestrel hangs perfectly still.

small falcon, with **long tail and pointed wings**; male has spotted, reddish-brown back, grey head and tail, and pale, spotted underparts; female is brown with black markings; both have black band at tip of tail

hunts in the open; hovers above ground then drops onto prey, including rodents and large insects; perches on posts, telegraph wires and other obvious places

shrill *ki-ki-ki-ki-ki*

common, but declining; likes open areas with rough grassland – including motorway verges; nests in towns but seldom visits gardens

Sparrowhawk, Hobby, Merlin, Cuckoo

Sparrowhawk (28–38cm)

You may only glimpse this dashing hunter as it shoots past.

small and upright, with **long tail and short, broad wings**; white eyebrow gives fierce expression; male is grey above with reddish barring below; female is much bigger, brown above and barred below

secretive; flies fast and low with 'flap-flap-flap-glide' pattern; catches small birds in flight; on sunny days, soars high – often in circles – with wings and tail spread; uses hidden perches

chattering *kew-kew-kew* when nesting

common and increasing; nests in forests but often hunts in open country; often visits towns, cities and gardens

Kestrel, Goshawk, Cuckoo

This powerful falcon is the jet fighter of the bird world.

medium-sized with heavy body, shortish tail and broad-based, pointed wings; adults are blue-grey above, with **black head, white throat and cheeks, and black 'moustache'**; adults are barred below, young are streaked

hunts birds in flight; often dives ('stoops') onto prey from great height; flies fast with quick wingbeats or circles high up; perches on cliffs and tall buildings

harsh, cackling *kek-rek-rek* when nesting

breeds in hilly areas of north and west and on rocky sea-cliffs; rare, but increasing; visits lowland areas in winter; may nest on tall buildings

Kestrel, Hobby, Merlin, Woodpigeon

SPEED KING

A diving Peregrine is probably the fastest bird in the world. Scientists think it can reach a speed of 240kph (150mph). But other birds may be faster than Peregrines in level flight – including the Eider Duck, timed at 75kph (47mph).

Even dragonflies are on the menu for this agile falcon.

Kestrel-sized, but with shorter tail and longer, more pointed wings; adults are blue-grey above, with black head, white throat and cheeks, and black 'moustache' (like Peregrine); streaked below (unlike adult Peregrine); **red on thighs and under tail**

hunts small birds and large insects in flight, often over water; may eat small prey in midair; often perches in isolated pine trees

shrill *kew-kew-kew* when nesting

uncommon summer visitor to England – especially south-east; also eastern Wales and southern Scotland; nests on lowland heaths and farmland with patches of trees

Kestrel, Peregrine, Cuckoo

BIRDS OF PREY IN FLIGHT

You will often see flying birds of prey from a distance. Look for their wing shape and any special markings to help identify them.

Golden Eagle
Huge; longer head than Buzzard; immatures have some white markings

Red Kite
Larger than Buzzard; angular wings; forked tail twists in flight

Buzzard
Broad wings and rounded tail; often soars and sometimes hovers

Osprey
Larger than Buzzard; white underneath; long narrow wings, like gull

Peregrine Falcon
Solid-looking; shortish tail and broad-based, pointed wings

Sparrowhawk
Short, broad wings; long tail; flies fast and low or soars high

Hobby
Narrow wings; fast, agile flight – almost like Swift

Kestrel
Pointed wings and long tail; hovers with fanned tail

♀ **Marsh Harrier**
Buzzard-sized, but slimmer; glides with wings held in 'V' shape

♂

You might disturb this game bird when tramping across moorland.

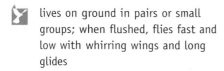
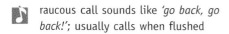

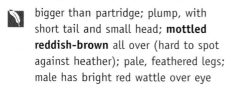 bigger than partridge; plump, with short tail and small head; **mottled reddish-brown** all over (hard to spot against heather); pale, feathered legs; male has bright red wattle over eye

lives on ground in pairs or small groups; when flushed, flies fast and low with whirring wings and long glides

raucous call sounds like *'go back, go back!'*; usually calls when flushed

upland areas of north and west; heather moorland away from trees

female Pheasant, partridges, Ptarmigan, Black Grouse, Capercaillie

Pheasant (53–89cm)

This colourful bird was introduced from Asia over 1,000 years ago.

large, with long neck; male is very colourful, with bottle-green head, bare, red face, copper underparts and **long, barred, orange tail;** some males have white neck-ring; female is pale brown with shorter (but still long) tail

walks slowly and deliberately; runs when disturbed, or takes off with explosion of wingbeats; flies low with whirring wings and long glides; roosts in bushes

raucous *ko-kok* call, while flapping wings

common on farmland and woodland edges, except in Scottish highlands; thousands are bred and released for hunting

partridges, grouse, Golden Pheasant

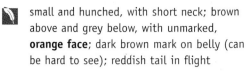

Grey Partridge (29–31cm)

This plump game bird is hard to spot as it crouches in a field.

CLUTCH CONTROL

The Grey Partridge lays one of the largest clutches of any bird in the world. It averages 15–19 eggs, but may even top 25. A female sometimes lays more than one clutch per season, in which case her second clutch is smaller.

small and hunched, with short neck; brown above and grey below, with unmarked, **orange face**; dark brown mark on belly (can be hard to see); reddish tail in flight

lives on ground in small groups; scratches for food with feet; prefers to crouch rather than fly; fast, low flight with whirring wings and long glides

grating *kerrick* call, especially at dusk

widespread, but not in hilly areas of north and west; open grassland and farmland with rough pasture and thick hedges

female Pheasant, young Red-legged Partridge, Corncrake, Quail

Red-legged Partridge (32–34cm)

This colourful partridge is easier to spot than its grey cousin.

slightly larger and less hunched than Grey Partridge; brown-and-grey plumage; **white throat-patch with black border**; black 'necklace' on breast; bold bars on flanks

feeds more out in open than Grey Partridge, and often in larger group; perches on vantage points such as posts; picks and scratches for food; runs when disturbed; flies like Grey Partridge

loud *chuck-chukka-chuck* call

common in southern, central and eastern England; also eastern Scotland and eastern Northern Ireland; open, dry farmland and woodland edges

female Pheasant, Grey Partridge, Corncrake, Quail

73

Look for a moorhen chugging around the edge of a pond.

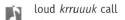

- smallish, plump water bird with up-tilted tail; dark brown and smoky grey, but looks black from a distance; **white line along flank and white under tail**; red forehead and red bill with yellow tip; young are pale below; long toes dangle in flight

- feeds on land and water, often near bank; usually alone or in small groups; swims with nodding head and flicking tail

- loud *krruuuk* call

- common, except in hilly areas and north-west Scotland; lakes, ponds, ditches and slow-flowing rivers

- Coot, Little Grebe (young)

Look out for this dumpy, black water bird on almost any large lake.

- larger than Moorhen, with rounder shape and shorter tail; **sooty black, with white bill and forehead**; young is pale below; long toes dangle in flight

- feeds mostly on water, often among other water birds; dives often; also feeds on bank; sometimes forms large flocks; quarrelsome – fights and chases rivals

- loud *kowk* call

- common, except in hilly areas and north-west Scotland; large open bodies of fresh water, such as park lakes and reservoirs

- Moorhen, Tufted Duck, grebes (young)

Oystercatcher (40–45cm)

This big, black-and-white wader is a noisy seaside resident.

large, stocky wader; black head, neck and upperparts, white underparts; white chin-strap in winter; **long, orange bill and pink legs**; in flight, white rump and wing-bars

Noisy and obvious; often flies about while calling; feeds along shore on shellfish, but doesn't wade deeply; also eats worms in fields; forms large flocks in winter

loud, high-pitched, piping *peep peep peep*

common all around coast; in northern regions also inland along river valleys; gathers in estuaries in winter

Avocet, Lapwing

Avocet (42–45cm)

This slim, elegant wader is our only bird with a fully upturned bill.

Oystercatcher-sized, but much slimmer, with longer neck and legs; mostly white, with black on crown, back of neck and back; **thin, upturned bill**; blueish legs; looks mostly white in flight

wades in shallow water; feeds by sweeping bill from side to side; often upends, may swim; very excitable – chases rivals and other birds; flocks in winter

piping *klute klute* call when alarmed

increasing – breeds in shallow coastal lagoons along coast of southern and south-eastern England; winters in south-west England

Oystercatcher, gulls (in flight), Black-winged Stilt (rare)

This colourful, noisy plover is most at home in fields and meadows.

 dove-sized, with long legs, short bill and **long crest**; dark green above and white below, with black markings on face and breast; broad, rounded wings, with pale wing-tips and white rump; flocks in flight flicker black and white

feeds on land with 'stop-run-peck' action; acrobatic flyer – dives and rolls during courtship display; mobs raptors and other birds; forms large winter flocks

loud, rolling *peewit* call

widespread on farmland and marshy areas; in winter on ploughed fields and along coast; breeding numbers are falling

Oystercatcher

Check the tideline carefully for hidden Ringed Plovers.

FooLED YOU!

Nesting Ringed Plovers use a trick called a 'distraction display' to fool predators that get too close. The plover limps away as though injured, dragging its wing and calling. The predator follows the adult, and so misses the nest.

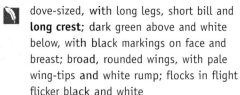

Little Ringed Plover: Like Ringed Plover, with yellow eye-ring and no wing-bar; inland summer visitor; passage visitor on coast.

small, plump wader with long legs and short bill; white below and sandy brown above; **black band around chest and across face** (fading to brown in winter); orange legs and black-tipped orange bill; narrow, white wing-bars in flight

usually alone or among groups of other small waders; feeds with 'stop-run-peck' action; freezes against background; fast, direct flight

two-note whistle, *too-lip* – usually in flight

common all around coast except south-west; sand and shingle beaches; uncommon inland

Little Ringed Plover, Sanderling

Grey Plover (27–30cm)

Scan carefully across an estuary: you can often spot a Grey Plover.

winter

solid shape with long legs and short bill; in winter, grey above and pale below with dark eye; in summer (rare in UK and Ireland), black face and belly; **in flight, black 'armpits' below**, white wing-bar and rump above

feeds alone or widely scattered, with typical plover 'stop-run-peck' action; often freezes; fast, direct flight

sorrowful whistle, *pee-uu-eee* – usually in flight

widespread around coast from autumn to spring, except in parts of northern Scotland and western Ireland; muddy and sandy shores; doesn't breed in UK

Golden Plover, Knot, Black-headed Gull (winter)

Golden Plover (26–29cm)

Look for this quiet bird among winter flocks of lapwings.

slimmer than Grey Plover, with finer bill; in summer, has **yellowish-brown back**, blackish underparts and broad, white line between; in winter, brownish breast and upperparts, and white belly; thin, white wing-bar in flight, but no black armpits

feeds on ground with typical plover 'stop-run-peck' action; forms large flocks – often with Lapwings; fast, direct flight

two-note whistle, *pu-wee* – usually in flight

uncommon breeding bird in boggy, upland regions of north and west; more widespread in winter, when large flocks gather on farmland and coastal marshes.

Grey Plover

winter

summer

Knot (23–25cm)

If you see one Knot, you'll probably see hundreds.

Flock in flight

- bigger than Dunlin, with shortish, straight bill; **greyish in winter**, with white belly and eyebrow; in summer (rare in UK and Ireland), brick-red below, with mottled black-and-grey back; white wing-bar in flight

- forms huge flocks (sometimes in thousands), which twist and turn in flight like shoals of fish; probes in mud for small shellfish

- soft *wutt-wutt* flight call

- winter and passage visitor to large estuaries and mudflats; uncommon inland; does not breed in UK

- Redshank, Dunlin, Grey Plover

winter

Sanderling (20–21cm)

This dinky little wader races along the beach like a clockwork toy.

NORTHERN NESTERS

Knot and Sanderling are among many waders that breed in the Arctic. This is why we seldom see their breeding colours or hear them singing. After breeding, they head south for winter. Some stay in the UK, but many travel much further – reaching South Africa, or even Australia.

winter

- small, hunched wader with short, straight bill; in winter, **white with grey back and dark mark on shoulder**; in summer (rare in UK and Ireland), reddish-brown breast and head and mottled back; in flight, white wing-bar and white sides to rump

- very energetic; small parties follow retreating waves to pick food from wet sand

- liquid whistle – *twick twick* – in flight

- winter and passage visitor to sandy beaches; rare on rocky coasts (including Scotland and south-west England); does not breed in UK

- Dunlin, Knot, Ringed Plover

Dunlin (16–20cm)

This little wader is often the most numerous in a mixed flock.

winter

summer

- sparrow-sized, with **slightly downcurved bill**; in winter, brownish-grey above and white below; in summer, reddish-brown back and black patch on belly; in flight, white wing-bar and white sides to rump

- may gather in huge flocks – often with other waders; flocks twist and turn in flight; probes mud and wades in shallow water

- short, grating flight call – *kreeet*

- in winter, common all round coast on muddy shores; in summer, smaller numbers breed on boggy upland areas in north and west; inland on passage

- Sanderling, Knot, Curlew Sandpiper, Purple Sandpiper

Turnstone (22–24cm)

Elaborate markings camouflage this chunky wader against the rocks.

- starling-sized wader with short, thick bill and orange legs; in summer, bold black and white pattern on face and breast, and black-and-orange pattern on back; in winter, mottled brown; **black, white and brown pattern striking in flight**

- small groups feed busily at water's edge, turning stones or seaweed; perches on posts; can be very tame

- chuckling *tuk-a-tuk-tuk* call in flight

- common around coast; prefers shores with rockpools and seaweed; does not breed in UK or Ireland; rare inland

- Ringed Plover, Oystercatcher (in flight)

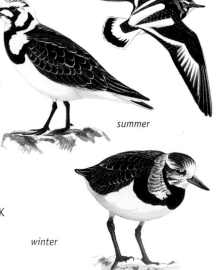

summer

winter

Curlew (50–60cm)

The lonely call of the Curlew drifts across estuaries all year round.

very big, gull-sized wader, with long neck and **very long, down-curved bill**; streaked greyish-brown all over; white rump and back in flight

feeds alone or in scattered groups; probes mud deeply; flocks at high-tide roost – often in fields; fluttering spring display flight, with long glides; looks a bit like gull in flight

lonely, rising *courleee* call; bubbling calls during display

common around coast in winter; in summer, breeds on upland areas in north and west – also on boggy lowland heaths in south

Whimbrel, godwits, young gulls

TooLS oF THE TRADE

Each type of wader has a bill suited to its own particular diet. This allows different species to feed together without competition. A Dunlin's short bill grabs small creatures near the water surface; a Curlew's long bill probes deep into mud for lugworms.

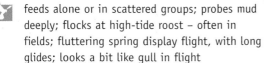

Bar-tailed Godwit (37–39cm)

You won't often see this wader's rich breeding colours in the UK.

large (but smaller than Curlew), with long neck and **long, slightly upturned bill**; in winter, greyish-brown above and pale below; in summer (rare in UK and Ireland), male has brick-red underparts; in flight, white rump and barred tail, but no wing-bars

usually feeds in small flocks, wading and probing mud; larger flocks at high-tide roost, often with other waders

low *kiruk, kiruk* call in flight

in winter, all around coast – though less common in south; prefers muddy shores and estuaries; does not breed in UK or Ireland

Black-tailed Godwit, Curlew, Whimbrel, Greenshank, Spotted Redshank

Black-tailed Godwit: longer legs and straighter bill than Bar-tailed; plainer grey in winter; in flight, black-and-white wings and black tail; winter visitor and rare breeder

Redshank (27–29cm)

This noisy wader is often first to spot danger and sound the alarm.

summer

winter

medium-sized, with medium-length bill and red legs; speckled brownish in summer, greyer in winter; in flight, white rump and back, and **broad, white band along rear edge of wing**

feeds alone or in small flocks; runs, wades and may swim; quickly takes flight when alarmed; often perches on posts; fluttering spring display flight; raises wings upon landing

ringing *teeu-tu-tu* alarm call; also yodelling *lew-lew-lew* during display

common on estuaries and salt marshes; also inland on marshes and moorland

Greenshank, Spotted Redshank, Green Sandpiper, Wood Sandpiper, Ruff

Greenshank (30–33cm)

Look for this elegant wader feeding busily at the back of a pool.

larger, slimmer and paler than Redshank, with **long neck, greenish legs and slightly upturned bill**; grey above and white below, with bolder markings in summer; in flight, white rump and back but no white on wings

usually feeds alone; walks fast, wades deeply and may swim; probes mud; sweeps bill from side to side like Avocet; fast, twisting flight

ringing three-part *tew-tew-tew* flight call

widespread but uncommon passage migrant to lakes, reservoirs and estuaries; breeds in northern Scotland on peat bogs

Redshank, Spotted Redshank, Green Sandpiper, Wood Sandpiper, Godwits, Ruff

winter

summer

81

Green Sandpiper (21–24cm)

Keep a lookout in autumn, when this shy wader is most common.

- smaller and dumpier than Redshank, with straight bill and greenish legs; dark breast and upperparts contrast with white belly; **in flight, white rump and dark underwings**

- usually in ones or twos; stays near cover; picks for food; often bobs rear end; takes off with fast zig-zag flight when flushed, like Snipe

- *tweet, weet-weet* flight call

- passage migrant to inland waters in southern half of England, Wales and Ireland; a few overwinter; gravel pits, ditches and marshy lakeshores

- Redshank, Wood Sandpiper, Common Sandpiper, Ruff

Common Sandpiper (19–21cm)

This busy little wader rarely stops bobbing up and down.

- smaller than Green Sandpiper, with more crouching posture; brown head and upperparts; **brown breast contrasts sharply with white belly**; in flight, thin, white wing-bar but no white rump

- usually alone or in pairs; bobs up and down constantly; often perches on rocks; flies low over water with quick beats of down-curved wings

- shrill *swee-wee-wee-wee* flight call

- summer visitor to rivers and streams in hilly regions of north and west; passage visitor to lowland sites including gravel pits and sheltered coasts; some overwinter

- Green Sandpiper, Wood Sandpiper, Dunlin

Ruff (20–30cm)

Look carefully: a 'puzzling' wader in autumn might well be a Ruff.

summer

♂

♀

 male is Redshank-sized, female is smaller; small head and short bill; at most times, brownish-grey with **scaly pattern on back**; breeding male has colourful ruff of feathers around head and neck; in flight, thin, white wing-bar and white sides to rump

 feeds singly or in small groups; picks at mud; lazy-looking flight; in spring, males gather to perform courtship displays (called leks)

 mostly silent – except during courtship

 passage visitor to lakes and coastal lagoons; rare breeding bird in East Anglia; some overwinter

 Green and Wood Sandpipers, Redshank, Greenshank

Snipe (25–27cm)

Camouflage markings make this secretive wader very hard to spot.

 medium sized, with round body, short legs and **very long, straight bill**; complex pattern of stripes and bars

 feeds alone or in small groups, seldom out in open; probes deeply into mud; flies off in fast zig-zag when flushed; in spring display flight, male vibrates outer tail feathers to make bleating sound (called 'drumming')

 squaatch alarm call when flushed; 'drumming' sounds like sheep high overhead

 widespread but not common breeding bird in bogs and marshes; more common in winter; prefers marshy ground at water's edge

 Green Sandpiper, Jack Snipe, Woodcock

FLEXIBLE FRIEND

A Snipe's long bill looks as stiff and brittle as a twig. But the tip is actually sensitive and flexible, and can open under the mud. This helps the Snipe to find hidden food such as worms and insect larvae.

Black-headed Gull (34–37cm)

This common small gull is often found far from the sea.

- smallish gull; bill and legs red in spring, white underparts, grey upperparts; head chocolate-brown in spring, otherwise white with dark smudges; in flight, **white stripe along front edge of wing**; young have ginger-brown markings

- usually moves in flocks; nests in colonies; 'paddles' with feet to stir up food; sits on water; catches insects in flight; follows ploughs

- harsh *keyaar* call; very noisy at colonies

- widespread inland or along coast; breeds on beaches and islands; common in winter on school playing fields and rubbish dumps

- Little Gull, Mediterranean Gull, Common Gull, Kittiwake (young)

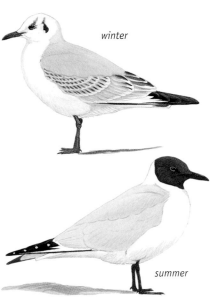

winter

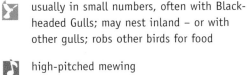

summer

Common Gull (40–42cm)

Despite its name, this gull is less common than some others.

winter

summer

- larger than Black-headed Gull; **greenish-yellow legs and bill** and dark eye; white head and underparts and grey upperparts; in winter, brown speckled head and neck; grey wings have black tips with white spots

- usually in small numbers, often with Black-headed Gulls; may nest inland – or with other gulls; robs other birds for food

- high-pitched mewing

- breeds along the coast and in upland regions in Scotland, northern England and western Ireland; more common in winter; often on playing fields

- Little Gull, Black-headed Gull, Mediterranean Gull, Kittiwake (young)

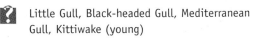

Kittiwake (38–40cm)

Of all our gulls, the Kittiwake is the only real 'sea' gull.

graceful, medium-sized gull; dark eye, small yellow bill and short, black legs; white head and underparts and grey upperparts; young have black 'W' pattern on wings; in flight, wings show two tones of grey; **neat, black wing-tips** have no white spots

breeds in big sea-cliff colonies – occasionally on dockside buildings; may follow fishing boats; never visits fields, parks or rubbish dumps

yowling calls at nest

breeds on steep sea-cliffs all around coast; spends winter far out at sea; rare inland

Common Gull, Herring Gull, Black-headed Gull (young), Fulmar

Herring Gull (55–67cm)

This noisy bird is a common sight in seaside towns.

large, with **fierce expression and heavy, yellow bill with red spot**; white, with grey back and wings; pink feet and yellow eyes; head flecked grey in winter; broad wings with white border and white spots on black tips; young are brown all over

nests in colonies on roofs and cliffs; joins mixed gull roosts; follows boats; raids bins in towns; sometimes aggressive; flocks fly high in formation

various loud mewing and wailing cries

common around coast all year and inland in winter

Common Gull, Lesser and Greater Black-backed Gulls (especially young)

RED MARKS THE SPOT

The red spot on a Herring Gull's bill is a target for its hungry chicks. When they peck this spot, the adult opens its bill and releases food into their mouths. The chicks' instinct is so strong that they will even peck the red spot on a plastic model.

Lesser Black-backed Gull (52–67cm)

This close relative of the Herring Gull often nests near its cousin.

- very similar in size and shape to Herring Gull, but with **yellow legs and slate-grey back and wings**; head flecked grey in winter; long wings narrower than Herring Gull's, with smaller white spots on black tips; young are brown all over

- nests in colonies; has wide diet and adapts to town life just like Herring Gull; joins mixed gull roosts

- mewing like Herring Gull, but deeper

- breeds around coast and on upland moors; widespread inland in winter; visits ploughed fields and rubbish dumps

- Herring Gull, Great Black-backed Gull (especially young)

Great Black-backed Gull (64–78cm)

This powerful seabird is the king of gulls.

- biggest gull, with massive, yellow bill and sturdy, pink legs; **blacker back and broader wings** than lesser Black-backed Gull; head flecked grey in winter; young are brown all over; in heavy flight can look almost like heron

- feeds like other large gulls, but hunts more live prey – including smaller seabirds; nests singly or in colonies; joins mixed gull roosts

- gruff bark – *uk–uk-uk*

- breeds on rocky coasts and islands in north and west; also on large lakes; widespread inland in winter; visits ploughed fields and rubbish dumps

- Lesser Black-backed Gull (especially young), Heron (in flight)

GULLS IN FLIGHT

Each gull has a different wing pattern, which helps you to identify it in flight. Remember that young gulls are much browner.

Lesser Black-backed Gull (adult)
Herring Gull-sized; usually dark grey (not black) back.

Great Black-backed Gull (adult)
Very big; very black above

Herring Gull (first winter)
Brown all over; looks like young black-backed gulls

Herring Gull (adult)
Grey back; black and white wing tips

Kittiwake (adult)
Silver-grey back; neat black wing tips with no white spots

Kittiwake (first winter)
Bold black 'W' shape across back and wings

Common Gull (adult)
Similar to Herring Gull, but smaller

Common Gull (first winter)
Brown and grey markings above; speckled head

Black-headed Gull (first winter)
Black and brown markings above; no black head

Black-headed Gull (adult, breeding)
White flash down front of wings; fine black wing tips

Little Gull (adult, non-breeding)
No black wing tips; dark underwings

Common Tern (31–35cm)

This typical tern looks lighter and more delicate than any gull.

winter

summer

smaller than Black-headed Gull, with longer, narrower wings and long, forked tail; white, with silver-grey upperparts and black cap; **pointed, red bill with black tip**; very short, red legs; darkish patch on primaries; white forehead in winter

light, bouncy flight, with head pointed down; sometimes hovers, before diving; never swims; often perches on posts; nests in colonies

high-pitched, grating *keee-yaaarr*

widespread summer visitor to coast and inland; uncommon in Wales and south-west England; nests on beaches and islands

Arctic Tern, Roseate Tern, Black-headed Gull, Little Gull

Arctic Tern (33–35cm)

This coastal bird migrates further than any other bird in the world.

AIR MILES

The Arctic Tern migrates further than any other bird. Each year, some fly all the way from their Arctic breeding grounds to their Antarctic wintering grounds and back again. An Arctic Tern that lives for 25 years may cover more than one million kilometres in its lifetime.

winter

summer

just like Common Tern, but with even lighter build, **longer tail and all-red bill**; soft, grey underparts make white cheeks stand out; dark line (not patch) along tips of primaries

flies like Common Tern, but more fluttery; often hovers in stages, before diving from quite low; nests in colonies

like Common Tern, but higher-pitched

summer visitor to northern and western coasts – especially Scottish islands; nests on islands and beaches; rare inland; spends winter at sea

Common Tern, Roseate Tern, Black-headed Gull, Little Gull

Sandwich Tern (36–41cm)

The earliest Sandwich Terns reach the UK coast late in February.

winter

summer

largest tern, with shortest tail, heaviest bill and whitest plumage; black cap has shaggy crest in spring, white forehead in winter; **thick, black bill with yellow tip**; short, black legs; long, angular wings

breeds in colonies, fishes in smaller groups; stronger and often higher flight than other terns; dives with splash (like small gannet)

harsh *ki-rrrick*; noisy

summer visitor to scattered breeding colonies around coast; nests on beaches and islands; widespread on passage; rare inland

Common Tern, Arctic Tern, Roseate Tern, small gulls

Little Tern (22–24cm)

This dainty little tern is one of our smallest seabirds.

smallest tern, with shortish, forked tail, large head and long bill; white, with grey back; **black cap has white forehead all year**; yellow bill has fine, black tip; very short, orange legs; narrow wings

breeds in small colonies – usually in smaller numbers than other terns; flies with fast wingbeats; hovers and dives constantly

shrill *krik–krik*

uncommon summer visitor to scattered coastal breeding colonies – mostly in south-east and eastern England; nests on sandy and shingle beaches; rare inland

Common Tern, Arctic Tern, Black Tern (winter)

winter

summer

Guillemot (38–41cm)

This upright seabird looks a little like a small penguin.

Woodpigeon-sized, with short tail, long neck and pointed bill; **white below, with chocolate brown head and upperparts**; some have white eye-ring; face and throat white in winter

breeds in dense sea-cliff colonies; perches on ledges, swims like a duck; dives from surface to catch fish; small wings look blurred in fast, low flight

growling calls at nest

breeds on steep sea-cliffs; most colonies in north and west, none in south-east; rest of the year at sea (usually in flocks), anywhere around coast

Razorbill, Puffin, Black Guillemot, sea ducks, divers (winter)

summer

winter

Razorbill (37–39cm)

You can often spot Razorbills among large crowds of Guillemots.

summer

winter

size and shape of Guillemot, but with larger head and broad bill flattened like blade; **black upperparts** (Guillemots are brown), with fine, white bar on wing, face and bill; face and throat white in winter

breeds on sea-cliffs; perches on ledges or swims like duck – with tail more cocked than Guillemot; dives very deeply; fast, low flight

growling calls at nest

breeds on steep sea cliffs with Guillemots; spends rest of year at sea, but less common inshore than Guillemot

Guillemot, Puffin, Black Guillemot, sea ducks

Puffin (26–29cm)

A colourful bill and comical expression make this a popular bird.

summer

THE EEL DEAL

The small silver fish that Puffins carry in their bills are called sand eels. They are the most important food for Puffins and many other seabirds during the breeding season. When sand eels die out, so do Puffins.

winter

- smaller than pigeon; **huge, colourful bill**; white below and black above; pale grey cheeks; clown markings around eye; red legs and feet; in winter, darker face and smaller bill

- nests in colonies on grassy cliffs; perches near burrow or swims on sea, diving often; carries beakfuls of small fish to nest; fast, direct flight – like huge bumble bee

- growling calls at nest

- breeds on rocky coasts and islands; most common in north and west Scotland; also Wales, Ireland, north-east and south-west England; rest of the year at sea

- Razorbill, Guillemot, Black Guillemot

Black Guillemot (30–32cm)

This auk is the least sociable and most northerly of its family.

- smaller and plumper than guillemot; in summer, **black all over with oval white patch on wing**; in winter, white below and mottled grey above; bright red legs and feet; wing-patches always show in flight

- usually in ones and twos; breeds in small colonies among boulders; swims like duck and dives deeply; fast, low flight, like Guillemot

- whistling *peeeee* at nest

- rocky coast of north and west Scotland and Ireland (rare in England and Wales); spends winter on sea, close to breeding sites

- Guillemot, Razorbill, Puffin, small grebes (in winter)

summer

winter

This unusual bird has a good reason for its secretive behaviour.

looks like small bird of prey, with pointed wings and long tail; grey upperparts, head and breast; white belly with black barring; rounded tail with white tip; thin, curved bill; young are brown, heavily barred

usually alone; lays eggs in other birds' nests (including Dunnock, Meadow Pipit and Reed Warbler); often mobbed by other birds; flies low, with wings beating below body; calls in flight or perched; wings droop below tail when perched

loud *cuc-koo* in spring; female makes bubbling calls

widespread summer visitor; moorland, farmland, reedbeds and coasts

Kestrel, Sparrowhawk, pigeons

A PERFECT MATCH

A Cuckoo's eggs always match the colour of its host's eggs. For instance, an egg laid in a Dunnock's nest is pale blue, while one laid in a Reed Warbler's nest is speckled brown. This way, the host never spots the extra egg – even though it's larger than its own.

This common city bird comes in many different plumages.

medium-sized pigeon; variable pattern of black, white, brown and grey – often with green or purple sheen on neck; **usually has white rump and black wing-bars**; wings white underneath

forms big flocks in towns; feeds on ground; roosts and nests on buildings; clatters wings on take-off; flies fast; glides and wheels with wings raised; very tame

bubbling and cooing calls during display

very common in many built-up areas; also cliffs, quarries and farmland.

Collared Dove, Stock Dove, Woodpigeon

Woodpigeon (40-42cm)

Our biggest pigeon is also one of our most common birds.

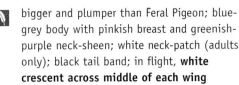

 bigger and plumper than Feral Pigeon; blue-grey body with pinkish breast and greenish-purple neck-sheen; white neck-patch (adults only); black tail band; in flight, **white crescent across middle of each wing**

 sometimes alone, but forms big flocks during winter; feeds in trees and on ground; clatters wings on take-off; in spring display, male flies up from trees, claps wings above back, then glides down

 rhythmic five-part cooing, *coo-ROO-roo, oo-roo*

 very common in woods, parks and gardens; in winter, mostly on farmland

 Collared Dove, Stock Dove, Feral Pigeon

Stock Dove (32-34cm)

This farmland bird is easily overlooked.

 size and shape of Feral Pigeon; blue-grey body with greenish neck-sheen and pale rump; two short, black wing-bars near body, and black tail-band; dark eye; wings grey underneath in flight; **no white markings**

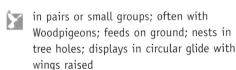 in pairs or small groups; often with Woodpigeons; feeds on ground; nests in tree holes; displays in circular glide with wings raised

 soft two-part cooing, *ooo-woo, ooo-woo*

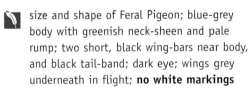 widespread, except northern Scotland and Northern Ireland; parkland and woodland edges with old trees; often feeds on farmland

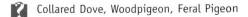 Collared Dove, Woodpigeon, Feral Pigeon

Turtle Dove (26–28cm)

The purring call of this summer visitor has become a rare sound.

- our smallest dove; slim, with diamond-shaped tail; blue-grey head, pink breast and **orange-brown back with black 'scales'**; black-and-white neck-patch; in flight, pale grey on wings and broad, white band across end of tail

- in pairs or small groups, often in tree canopy; feeds on ground; in spring display, male flies up, claps wings, then glides down with tail fanned

- cat-like purring, often from hidden perch

- uncommon summer visitor, mostly to south and east England; open woods, parkland, and farmland with thick hedges

- Collared Dove, Feral Pigeon

Collared Dove (31–33cm)

This common bird only started breeding in the UK in 1955.

- slimmer and longer-tailed than Feral Pigeon; pale greyish-brown body; **thin, black bar either side of neck**; in flight, broad, white band at end of tail

- often in pairs, seldom in flocks; feeds on ground; sings from roofs and wires; in spring display, flies steeply up, then glides down with wings fanned

- loud, rhythmic, three-part cooing, *coo-COO-coo*

- common everywhere except upland areas; likes gardens and farms, but avoids city centres; often visits bird tables

- Woodpigeon, Feral Pigeon, Turtle Dove

Barn Owl (33–35cm)

Look out at dusk for a ghostly white shape drifting over the fields.

smaller and slimmer than Tawny Owl; **snow-white underparts**; honey and soft grey upperparts; big head with heart-shaped face; long legs; long, rounded wings

usually alone; hunts mostly at dusk, sometimes also by day; flies slowly over fields in search of rodents; often hovers; nests in old farm buildings and sometimes on cliffs

eerie shrieks and hissing screams

widespread but uncommon; absent from parts of northern Scotland and western Ireland; rough farmland, woodland edges and coastal marshes; often near ditches and riverbanks

Tawny Owl, Short-eared Owl, gulls (in flight)

Tawny Owl (37–39cm)

Often heard, but seldom seen, this is the original 'brown owl'.

large, stocky (Woodpigeon-sized) with big head; short, broad wings; **reddish-brown upperparts marked with white**; heavily streaked underparts; ring around face; white markings between dark eyes

usually alone; hunts at night and roosts in tree by day; swoops on rodents from perch; nests in holes; rarely seen by day unless flushed; often mobbed by small birds at roost; fast, silent flight

wavering hoot, *hoo-hoo-hoo*; female makes high shriek – *kee-wick*

widespread everywhere except Ireland; deciduous and coniferous woodland, parks, gardens and churchyards

Barn Owl, Long-eared Owl, Short-eared Owl

Little Owl (21–23cm)

This pocket predator is the smallest of our owls.

- very small (Starling-sized), with large, square head and short tail; rounded wings. greyish-brown upperparts with white spots; heavily streaked underparts; fierce-looking, **yellow eyes with white eyebrows**

- usually alone; hunts at night, but often seen by day; hunts small mammals and insects – also earthworms on ground; often perches on post out in open; nests in holes; undulating flight

- high-pitched shriek – *kiew kiew kiew*

- widespread in England, Wales and southern Scotland (not Ireland); farmland with woods, hedgerows and old trees

- Tawny Owl

Short-eared Owl (37–39cm)

You might spot this owl out hunting by day.

- slimmer and smaller-headed than Tawny Owl; small 'ear' tufts hard to see; brown and streaky all over; yellow eyes with dark borders; in flight, **long wings pale below with dark bar at 'wrist'**

- usually alone, but may roost in groups; hunts at dawn and dusk; flies low in search of prey; may glide like harrier; usually perches on ground or fence posts

- low *hoo-hoo-hoo-hoo*, but usually silent

- uncommon; breeds in northern and eastern England, Wales and Scotland; more widespread in winter; open country, including moorland and coastal marshes

- Barn Owl, Long-eared Owl, harriers.

A loud call and a flash of green usually give this bird away.

♀

TIP of THE TONGUE

A woodpecker's amazing tongue is longer than its head and bill combined. It is rooted right at the back of the skull, and shoots out to capture small creatures hidden deep in holes. Tiny sticky barbs on the tip stop the prey from escaping.

♂

biggest woodpecker, with pointed bill and short, pointed tail; green above and greyish below; black face markings (with red in male) and red crown; in flight, **yellowish-green rump**

usually alone; on ground, digs for ants with bill; in trees, hops jerkily up trunk with tail pressed against bark and taps for food; nests in tree holes; bounding flight with bursts of flapping

loud, laughing *klu-klu-klu-klu* – often in flight

widespread except Ireland and north-west Scotland; open woodland and parkland; often feeds on lawns

Great Spotted Woodpecker, Mistle Thrush, Golden Oriole (female)

Great Spotted Woodpecker (22–23cm)

This bark-basher often scatters other birds from the feeder.

Song Thrush-sized, with pointed bill and tail; black-and-white face and upperparts, with white oval on shoulder; cream below, with **red under tail**

♀

usually alone; climbs tree trunk with tail pressed against bark; taps and probes for food; hangs from birdfeeders; may raid nestboxes for nestlings; bounding flight, with short bursts of flapping; seldom visits ground

loud *tchik!* call; in spring, drums bill against tree trunk in short, loud bursts

common anywhere with trees, except Ireland and northern Scotland; woods, parks and large gardens

Lesser Spotted Woodpecker, Green Woodpecker

♂

A blur of blue may be all you see when a Kingfisher flashes past.

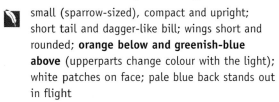 

small (sparrow-sized), compact and upright; short tail and dagger-like bill; wings short and rounded; **orange below and greenish-blue above** (upperparts change colour with the light); white patches on face; pale blue back stands out in flight

shy; usually alone; perches quietly on overhanging branch; dives underwater to catch fish; sometimes hovers; flies fast and low; nests in riverbank tunnel

sharp, high-pitched *zeee*, or *zee-teee* in flight

widespread, except northern Scotland and western Ireland; slow-flowing rivers, lakes, canals in built-up areas; visits estuaries in winter

dipper (call and flight)

This high speed daredevil hardly ever leaves the air.

AIR FLAIR

Swifts are true flying champions. They feed, mate and even sleep on the wing. Young Swifts born in Europe fly to Africa and back at least twice before they are ready to breed. They may spend three years in flight without landing once.

larger than Swallow, with small body and thin, curved wings; **crescent-shaped in flight**; blackish-brown with pale throat; looks paler in sunlight; short, forked tail; bill almost invisible

feeds in midair on tiny insects; flies very fast, with stiff, flickering wingbeats and long glides; in spring, noisy groups chase each other; gathers high up in flocks; only lands at nest site (usually on old, tall building); flies low before storms

harsh, screaming *screeeeee*; flying groups call together

common summer visitor everywhere except northern Scotland; often above towns and lakes

Swallow, House Martin, Sand Martin

Swallow (17–19cm)

Soon after leaving the nest, young Swallows set out for Africa.

smaller than Swift, with **long tail streamers** and more flexible wings; blue-black upperparts and breast-band, white underparts and red face; in flight, white 'windows' in tail; young have shorter tail

feeds on insects in air; agile flight, but not as high as Swift; flies low over water and may touch surface; perches on wires, where flocks gather in autumn; nests in farm buildings

light *vit vit* call; long, twittering song

common summer visitor; farmland, villages, ponds; not city centres

Swift, House Martin, Sand Martin

House Martin (12.5cm)

This small relative of the Swallow shares its home with people.

smaller and more compact than Swallow, with shorter, forked tail; blue-black upperparts and entirely white underparts; **white rump** in flight; young are browner

darting flight, like Swallow's, but more fluttery and often higher up; perches on wires and roofs; small colonies nest under eaves of buildings; lands on ground to gather mud for nest

priit flight call; soft, twittering song

summer visitor everywhere except north-west Scotland; nests in towns and villages, but not city centres

Sand Martin, Swallow, Swift

99

This riverbank nester is one of our earliest summer visitors.

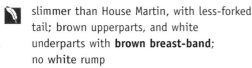

- slimmer than House Martin, with less-forked tail; brown upperparts, and white underparts with **brown breast-band**; no white rump

- flies like House Martin; catches insects in air – mostly over water; perches on wires; small colonies dig nest holes in sandbanks; flocks roost in reedbeds

- rattling twitter – harsher than House Martin

- summer visitor everywhere except far north-west Scotland; more localised than House Martin; feeds near nest sites – beside rivers or in quarries; flocks use reservoirs and reedbeds in autumn

- House Martin, Swallow, Swift

SPREADING SANDS

Fewer and fewer Sand Martins are visiting Europe. Their numbers may be falling because their winter quarters in Africa are shrinking. Farming and climate change is causing the Sahara Desert to expand, leaving many areas too dry for Sand Martins.

Skylark (18–19 cm)

You have to scan the skies to spot this springtime songster.

- slightly larger than sparrow, with **short crest** (not always raised); brown above and pale below; streaked breast and upperparts; in flight, white outer tail feathers and white edge to back of rounded wings

- feeds on ground; crouches when alarmed; flies up slowly to great height, then gradually descends, singing non-stop; forms large flocks in winter

- liquid *chirrup* call; continuous, warbling song

- common on farmland, grassland and upland areas; winter flocks in fields and along coast

- Woodlark, Meadow Pipit, Tree Pipit, buntings

Meadow Pipit (14.5 cm)

Up on the moors this is often the only small bird around.

Display flight

- smaller and more upright than Skylark, with thinner bill and no crest; brown above and pale below; streaked back and breast; **white outer tail feathers**

- walks with wagging tail; often flutters around while calling; flies up in display flight (not nearly as high as Skylark), then parachutes down

- thin, whistled call, *see-see-see*; song is run of high notes accelerating to trill

- common and widespread in open country and upland regions; winter flocks in fields and along coast – sometimes with Skylarks

- Tree Pipit, Rock Pipit, Skylark, Woodlark

Rock Pipit (16.5–17 cm)

You might spot this pipit foraging among seaweed like a wader.

- larger and darker than Meadow Pipit; brown above and pale below, with **smudgy, streaked underparts**; dark legs and bill; grey outer tail feathers

- walks, hops and runs along shore; perches on prominent rocks; display flight like Meadow Pipit; often quite tame

- single whistle, *pseep*; song like Meadow Pipit, but stronger

- widespread on rocky coasts; uncommon in south-east England; feeds along shoreline and at base of cliffs; rare inland

- Meadow Pipit, Water Pipit, Skylark, Shore Lark

Pied Wagtail (18cm)

This busy insect-catcher is a common bird about town.

sparrow-sized; **black and white with long tail**; black crown and bib; white face and belly; male has black back, female grey; young are browner, with brown breast-band

usually feeds alone; walks and runs, wagging tail constantly; chases insects energetically; bounding flight; large roosts gather in town centres

sharp *chizik* flight call; simple, twittering song

common and widespread in open country, including towns; often (but not always) near water; likes roofs, lawns, car parks and school playgrounds

Grey Wagtail, Yellow Wagtail (young), pipits (young)

Yellow Wagtail (17cm)

This summer visitor has a shorter tail than other wagtails.

shorter tail than Pied Wagtail; male **green above, with yellow face and underparts**; female duller; young has brownish 'necklace' on throat

runs like other wagtails, with constantly wagging tail; often feeds around feet of cattle; flutters after flying insects; small flocks gather on migration; bounding flight

loud *pseet* call, in flight or perched

summer visitor to England and southwest Scotland, but not Ireland; lowland farmland – especially marshes and water meadows; breeds near water; visits playing fields on migration

Grey Wagtail, Pied Wagtail (young)

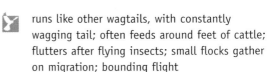

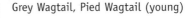
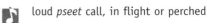

Look out for this wagtail beside water in the town or country.

♀

♂

summer

similar size to Pied Wagtail, with even longer tail; summer male is **yellow below, with grey back, black throat** and white eyebrow; female and winter male have pale throat and yellow only under tail

often in pairs; runs like other wagtails, with wagging tail; perches on rocks in water; bounding flight, low over water

sharp *tswik* flight call – shorter than Pied Wagtail

widespread; in summer, upland streams and rivers with weirs; in winter, lowland ponds, canals and even city roof tops

Pied Wagtail, Yellow Wagtail

Dipper (18cm)

This is the only bird that walks underwater along the riverbed.

plump body and cocked tail (like big Wren); adults **blackish-brown, with white bib** and chestnut belly; young grey above and pale below; short, rounded wings

usually alone or in pairs; perches on rocks in stream, then ducks underwater to feed; bobs constantly; takes off when disturbed; disappears around bend of river in low, buzzing flight; often nests under bridges

sharp *zit zit* flight call; soft, warbling song

upland regions, mostly in north and west; fast-flowing rivers or edges of upland lakes; follows rivers into towns during winter

Wren, Kingfisher (call and flight)

> **DIVING GEAR**
>
> *The Dipper is the only songbird that can feed completely underwater. It sees through transparent eyelids, and a special membrane of skin keeps its nostrils closed until it surfaces again.*

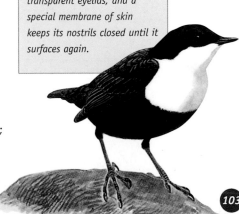

103

Wren (9–10cm)

You might sometimes mistake this tiny little bird for a mouse.

tiny, with cocked tail and sharp bill; very short, rounded wings; warm brown above, with fine barring and pale eyebrow; paler below

feeds alone; creeps about busily in roots, walls and low vegetation; in fast, buzzing flight looks like big bee; sings from raised perch; may roost huddled together

sharp, scolding *tik tik* call; loud, rattling song, usually ending in a trill

very common; almost every habitat – with or without trees; likes ivy and old walls

Dipper (young), Dunnock, Goldcrest, mouse

SPARE NESTS

A male Wren does his best to impress a female by building several nests. The female chooses just one in which to lay her eggs. If she has a second brood, she may use one of the spares. The rest are all abandoned.

Dunnock (14.5cm)

This quiet little bird usually keeps a low profile around the garden.

Wing-flicking display

sparrow-sized, with thinner bill; brown above, with black streaks; **blue-grey face and breast**; no eyebrow or pale markings

usually feeds alone; shuffles along close to ground, near cover; flicks wings; sings from prominent perch in bush or low tree; bullied by Robins at bird table

piping *tseep* call; short, fast, warbling song

very common; almost everywhere except mountain-tops; likes mixed woodland, gardens, thickets and hedges

House Sparrow (female), Robin (young), Wren

Stonechat (12.5cm)

This restless, noisy little bird usually makes itself very obvious.

summer

♂

♀

summer

♂

♀

smaller than Robin, with big, round head; summer male has **black head, white half-collar and orange breast**; female and winter male are duller; in flight, white rump and wing-patches

often in pairs; perches upright on top of low tree or bush, especially gorse; calls and flicks wings; drops down to feed

call, *hweet, chak-chak* – like stones struck together; warbling song like Dunnock's

most common in north and west; moorland, heathland and coastal areas with gorse and heather; often on golf courses

Wheatear, Whinchat, Redstart, Robin

Wheatear (14.5–15.5cm)

A flash of white rump often reveals this early summer visitor.

larger than Robin, with upright shape and short tail; spring male is blue-grey above, pinkish-orange below, with black wings, black ear-coverts and white eyebrow; female and autumn male are browner; in flight, **bold white rump and white tail with black 'T-bar'**

feeds on ground alone or in pairs; runs after insects in short bursts; perches on rock or post; bobs up and down

hard *chak-chak*, like Stonechat; warbling song

summer visitor, mostly to north and west; rocky moorland and upland pastures; coastal dunes and grassland; widespread on passage

Whinchat, Stonechat

105

Robin (14cm)

This garden favourite can be less friendly than you might think.

- sparrow-sized, with upright stance, big head and thin bill; **orange-red breast and face** and brown upperparts, with blue-grey line between; whitish belly; young are mottled brown

- usually feeds alone; hops along ground or drops down from low perch (branch, post, spade handle); cocks tail; sings from high perch; rivals chase each other and fight

- urgent *tic tic* call; sweet, liquid, high-pitched song all year round, sometimes at night

- very common and widespread; woodland edges, hedgerows, parks and gardens; usually feeds near cover

- Dunnock, Redstart, Black Redstart, Nightingale

> **SEEING RED**
>
> Male Robins fight fiercely over territory. The red breast of one acts as a trigger for its rival to attack. Young Robins start life with a speckled brown breast. This keeps them safe from attack until they find a territory of their own.

Redstart (14cm)

'Start' is an old word for tail, this bird's most striking feature.

♀

♂

summer

- slimmer than Robin; spring male has blue-grey upperparts, black face and throat, white forehead and orange breast; female and autumn male are brownish above and pale orange below; young are mottled like young Robin; all have **orange-red tail and rump**

- flits through trees after insects; quivers tail; sings from high perch; seldom comes to the ground

- call, *hooeet* (like Willow Warbler); soft, warbly song

- Scotland, Wales and northern and western England (not Ireland); oak woodland and old pine forests; more widespread on migration

- Black Redstart, Robin, Nightingale

Look out for a flash of red tail on a city rooftop.

robin-sized; summer male is grey above and sooty-black below, with **white wing panels and an orange-red tail**; female, young and winter male are greyish-brown with an orange-red tail

hops around buildings and rocks, constantly quivering tail; sings from rooftops; may hover after insects like flycatcher

warbling song, ending in strange crunching noise (like gravel path); short *tak, tak* call

uncommon; central and southern England and Wales; nests in city wasteland and industrial areas; winters on sea cliffs; widespread around the coast on migration

Redstart, Robin, House Sparrow

'Black' only describes the male of this common garden songster.

larger and longer-tailed than Starling; male is **black with yellow bill**; female and young are dark brown with speckled throat and breast

feeds on ground; hops across lawn in bursts; stops to spot prey; rummages in leaf litter; tail jerks up when landing, then sinks slowly down; sings from prominent perch, such as bare tree or roof – sometimes at night; flies low into cover

many different calls, including shrill *chink chink chink*; rich, fluty song with many separate phrases

very common and widespread; woodland, parks and gardens

Starling, Ring Ouzel, Jackdaw

This garden bird is an expert snail smasher.

smaller than Blackbird; unmarked brown face and upperparts; pale, **spotted underparts with orangish underwing in flight**; young have pale, streaked upperparts

often alone; feeds quietly on ground – usually near cover; hops in bursts, stopping to spot prey; smashes open snail shells by banging them on stone; direct, straight flight; sings from high, prominent perch

thin, *tsic* flight call; loud, tuneful song, with many phrases, each repeated up to five times

common and widespread; parks, gardens, woodland and hedgerows

female Blackbird, Mistle Thrush, Redwing, Fieldfare, Starling

> **FRUIT SUPPLY**
>
> *Thrushes eat plenty of berries and other fruit. Try leaving out fallen fruit, such as apples, on the lawn. This can be a big help in hard winter weather, when other food is tricky to find. You may even attract Redwings or Fieldfares to your garden.*

Redwing (21cm)

Redwings arrive in October to enjoy the autumn berries.

slightly smaller than Song Thrush; brown upperparts, **cream eyebrow and stripe below cheek**; pale, spotted underparts; reddish flanks; reddish underwing in flight

shy; flocks feed on berries or (later in the winter) on the ground; often with Fieldfares and other thrushes; looks like Starling in fast flight

soft *seeep* flight call, often heard overhead at night in autumn; jumbled song when breeding

common and widespread winter visitor to farmland, parks, hedgerows and orchards; rare breeding bird in north Scotland

Song Thrush, Mistle Thrush, Fieldfare, Starling, female Blackbird

This bold, upright bird is the largest of our thrushes.

bigger than Blackbird and Song Thrush; greyish-brown upperparts; **whitish underparts with bold, round spots**; in flight, white tail-corners and pale rump

upright and obvious; often in pairs; feeds in open; strong, dipping flight (like woodpecker); may be aggressive towards other birds; sings from exposed perch, often in stormy conditions; early nester – high in tall tree

loud, rattling call; powerful, Blackbird-like song, with separate repeated phrases

common and widespread; open woodland and parkland with tall trees

Song Thrush, Fieldfare, female Blackbird, Green Woodpecker.

Fieldfare (25.5cm)

Each winter this handsome thrush visits the UK from Scandinavia.

slightly smaller than Mistle Thrush, with longer tail; reddish-brown back and wings, **grey head and rump**, and thickly-spotted orangish breast; in flight, grey rump contrasts with black tail

sociable; flocks feed in bushes or on ground; feeds with other birds, including Redwings, Starlings and Lapwings; loose flight – often high up; noisy flocks gather towards end of winter

chattering *chak, chak-chak* in flight; warbly song when breeding

common and widespread winter visitor; fields, parks, hedgerows and orchards; very rare breeding bird in north

Mistle Thrush, female Blackbird

A glimpse of stripy face quickly identifies this reedbed songster.

- slightly smaller than sparrow, with flattish head and fine bill; streaky brown above and pale below; dark crown and **bold, white eyebrow**; reddish-brown rump in flight

- clambers among tangled vegetation, often near base; pops up to sing from bush; performs short song flight

- scolding *chirr, chirr* call; long, chattering song, including sweet notes and chirrups; may mimic other birds' songs

- widespread and common summer visitor; mainly damp habitats, including reed-beds, ditches and waterside scrub

- Reed Warbler, Marsh Warbler (rare), Wren

SINGING FOR SUCCESS

Like all birds, a male Sedge Warbler sings to attract a female. His complicated song contains thousands of different notes, including many stolen from other birds. No two songs are ever the same. He stops singing as soon as a female arrives.

Even when singing loudly, this skulking warbler often stays hidden.

- same size as Sedge Warbler, with longer bill and peaked head; **plain brown above** and pale below with white throat and faint eyebrow; reddish-brown rump in flight

- climbs among reeds; often sings low down; builds nest on reed stems; favourite host for Cuckoo

- sharp *chrrr* alarm call; long, chattering song – more mechanical and less lively than Sedge Warbler

- summer visitor to England, Wales and eastern Ireland; most common in south and east; reedbeds on lakes, marshes and ditches

- Sedge Warbler, Marsh Warbler (rare)

Blackcap (13cm)

Berries provide winter food for this tuneful warbler.

♀

♂

size of Great Tit; male is brownish above and grey below, with **jet-black crown**; female and young are browner, with reddish-brown crown

feeds energetically in trees and bushes; eats fruit in autumn and visits bird tables in hard weather; sings from quite high up

harsh *tac*, and scolding *cherrr* calls; tuneful song, with rich, fluty phrases

widespread summer visitor, and all year in south; deciduous and mixed woodland, thickets, parks and large gardens

Garden Warbler (especially song), Whitethroat, Marsh Tit, Willow Tit

Whitethroat (14cm)

This perky summer songster often pops up on top of a bush.

size of Great Tit, with longish tail and peaked crown; male has brown back, reddish-brown wings and grey head; **white throat** contrasts with off-white underparts; female is browner, but also with white throat

forages in thick vegetation; pops up to sing from top of bush; often cocks tail; jerky song flight in spring

scolding *tac, tac* and *cherrr* calls; short, scratchy song

widespread summer visitor, except Scottish Highlands; hedgerows, scrub (especially gorse, hawthorn and brambles)

Lesser Whitethroat, Blackcap, Garden Warbler, Dartford Warbler

♀

♂

This warbler's lilting song quickly tells it apart from the Chiffchaff.

- very small (size of Blue Tit), slim and neat; greenish-brown above and yellowish-white below; dark eye-stripe and pale eyebrow; **pale legs**

- forages busily among leaves in tree canopy; moves about while singing from exposed branch; joins mixed feeding parties in autumn

- soft, repeated *hoo-eet* call; sweet song starts softly and ends with flourish

- very common and widespread summer visitor; forest edges and clearings, young plantations, birch woods, parks

- Chiffchaff, Wood Warbler

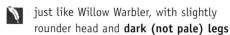

Chiffchaff (10–11cm)

This warbler's jerky song tells it apart from the Willow Warbler.

- just like Willow Warbler, with slightly rounder head and **dark (not pale) legs**

- forages like Willow Warbler, but more twitchy; moves about while singing from exposed branch; hovers to pick insects from leaf; joins mixed feeding parties

- *hweet* call, shorter than Willow Warbler's; bouncy two-note song – *chiff-chaff, chiff-chaff* – often repeated for a long time

- common and widespread summer visitor; woodland, parks and sometimes gardens; some overwinter in south

- Willow Warbler, Wood Warbler

Wood Warbler (12cm)

This is our yellowest warbler – usually seen high in the branches.

larger than Willow Warbler/Chiffchaff, with shorter tail, longer wing-tips and bigger-chested shape; green above with yellow eyebrow; **yellow breast and white belly**; brown legs

forages high in tree canopy; very agile; flutters and hovers to catch insects; does not flick tail; performs fluttering display flight among trees

sorrowful *pew-pew* call; high-pitched, silvery song that ends in trill

localised summer visitor, mostly to north and west; rare in south and east; oak woods in upland regions; sometimes beech woods

Willow Warbler, Chiffchaff

Goldcrest (9cm)

This tiny insect eater is the smallest bird in Europe.

tiny; short wings and needle-thin bill; greenish above and whitish below; **black-and-yellow stripe along crown** (orange centre not always visible); no eye-stripe; thin, white wing-bar; young has plain crown

always on the move; feeds high among branches, hovers beside leaves and may creep up trunk; joins mixed feeding parties; quite tame

very high-pitched *seee* call; weedling song – *tseedle-dee, tseedle-dee* – that speeds up into short trill

common and widespread; coniferous woodland, parks, gardens, churchyards with yew trees

Firecrest, Willow Warbler, Chiffchaff, Wren

HARD TIMES

Winter can be tough for Goldcrests. It's hard for these tiny birds to find food and survive the cold. More than a quarter of British Goldcrests may die during one very cold winter. But, after several mild winters, the population quickly rises again.

113

Spotted Flycatcher (14.5cm)

Look out for the aerial acrobatics of this expert insect catcher.

sparrow-sized, with peaked head and longish wings; greyish-brown above and pale below, with **streaks on breast and crown**; young have pale spots on upperparts

feeds by darting out from low perch to catch flying insects, often fluttering and hovering, then returning to same perch or another nearby; flicks wings while perched; often quite tame

thin *zeee* call; soft, warbly song

widespread but declining summer visitor; woodland glades, large parks and gardens with good mix of trees

Robin (young); Redstart; Pied Flycatcher

Pied Flycatcher (13cm)

This black-and-white woodland bird sometimes uses nest boxes.

♀

summer

♂

smaller and plumper than Spotted Flycatcher; summer male is white below and black above, with white forehead and **white wing-patches**; female and winter male are browner, but also with wing patches

catches insects like Spotted Flycatcher, but does not return to the same perch; flicks wings and cocks tail; nests in tree holes and may use nestboxes

sharp *huit* call; song a series of sweet notes

summer visitor to western England, south-west Scotland and Wales; deciduous woodland – especially hilly oak woods; widespread on migration

Spotted Flycatcher, Great Tit

Over two-thirds of this bird's length consists of its tail.

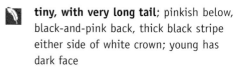

HELPING oUT

Long-tailed Tits are among the luckiest parents in the bird world. Youngsters from their previous year's brood often tag along to help them raise the new chicks. These 'helpers' may never breed themselves.

tiny, with very long tail; pinkish below, black-and-pink back, thick black stripe either side of white crown; young has dark face

feeds in small groups, which flit one by one from tree to tree; acrobatic – often hangs upside down; roosts huddled together in cold weather; visits bird tables

high-pitched *see see* call, with short hissing trills – *tsrrrrr, tsrrrrr*

common and widespread, except far northern Scotland; deciduous and mixed woodland, hedgerows, parks and gardens with plenty of cover

Pied Wagtail, Coal Tit, Bearded Tit

Coal Tit (11.5cm)

This little tit often flees when bigger birds arrive at the feeder.

smaller than Great Tit, with big head; dirty white below and greyish-brown above; black head and throat, with white cheeks and white stripe down nape; two white wing-bars; young are greenish-yellow

usually alone or in pairs; feeds acrobatically and high up, may hover, or search trunk like Treecreeper; joins mixed feeding parties; stores food to eat later

thin *see see* call; loud two-part song, *pee-chew, pee-chew*

common and widespread; mixed and coniferous woodland, parks and gardens – especially with conifers

Great Tit, Marsh Tit, Willow Tit

Blue Tit (11.5cm)

This acrobat of the bird feeder is a regular garden visitor.

smaller than Great Tit; blue-and-green above and yellow below (sometimes with thin, black belly-stripe); **white face with blue cap** and black line through eye; young are more greenish

feeds acrobatically on feeders and among outer branches, often hanging upside down; often dominates mixed feeding parties; nests in holes and nestboxes

thin *see see* call and churring alarm call, *see-see-see churrr*

very common and widespread; deciduous woodland (particularly oak), parks and gardens – including city centres

Great Tit, Coal Tit

CATERPILLAR CoLLECToRS

A pair of Blue Tits collects hundreds of caterpillars each day to feed its growing brood. By the time the chicks have fledged, they may have gobbled up over 10,000 caterpillars. No wonder the exhausted parents look so tatty!

Great Tit (14cm)

Our biggest and boldest tit has many different songs.

♀

♂

larger (sparrow-sized) and sleeker than other tits; green above with blueish wings; yellow below with **thick, black belly-stripe** (wider in male); black head with white cheeks; young are more greenish-yellow

busy visitor to birdfeeders; often feeds on ground; may cling to tree trunk and tap bark; joins mixed feeding parties; nests in holes and nestboxes

churring alarm, and sharp chink call like Chaffinch; different songs, all with see-saw rhythm, *tea-cher, tea-cher, tea-cher*

very common and widespread; woodland, farmland, parks and gardens

Blue Tit, Coal Tit

Only the agile Nuthatch can climb down trees headfirst.

- size of Great Tit, with short tail, big head and strong, pointed bill; rounded wings; blue-grey above and pinkish-orange below, with **bold black stripe though eye**

- climbs busily up and down tree trunk and along high branches; taps loudly on bark, hammering nuts and digging out insects; visits feeders and feeds on ground; packs mud around entrance to nest hole; stores food

- loud, repeated *dueet, dueet-dueet*; also *pee-pee-pee-pee* trill

- widespread in England and Wales; rare in Scotland, none in Ireland; mixed and deciduous woodland, farmland, parks and large gardens

- Blue Tit, Great Tit, Treecreeper, woodpeckers

This quiet bird climbs quite differently from the noisy Nuthatch.

- small and mousy, with pointed tail and **thin, down-curved bill**; streaky brown above with white eyebrow; clean white below; creamy wing-bars in flight

- never still; shuffles up (never down) tree trunks like mouse, often spiralling round, then flies to base of next tree and starts again; probes for insects with bill; roosts in bark crevices; joins mixed feeding parties; doesn't use feeders

- thin *tsee tsee* call; very high-pitched trilling song

- common and widespread (except some Scottish islands); coniferous and deciduous woodland, parks and large gardens

- Nuthatch, Wren, Lesser Spotted Woodpecker

Jay (34–35cm)

A flash of white rump quickly gives away this colourful crow.

 pigeon-sized, with longish tail and short, thick bill; pinkish grey, with black moustache and pale crest on forehead; black-and-white wings with bright blue patch; in flight, shows **broad, white rump** and rounded wings

hard to see; hops energetically on ground or through tree; buries acorns; raids birds' nests; visits birdtables and birdbaths; floppy, uneven flight – often one bird shortly behind another

loud, grating screech (carries far through woods)

widespread, except far northern Scotland and western Ireland; woodland (especially oak), parks and large gardens

Magpie, Hoopoe (rare)

Magpie (44–46cm)

This bold, long-tailed garden visitor finds a meal almost anywhere.

NoT GUILTY!

Some people blame Magpies for the decline of many garden birds. It's true that Magpies eat eggs and nestlings. But studies show that they don't affect songbird populations. The real problem for songbirds is lack of food and nesting habitat.

pigeon-sized; **black and white with strong bill and long tail**; black parts can shine green or blue; in flight, short, rounded wings show white patches on primaries

alone or in groups; wide diet; walks or hops boldly on ground – often with tail cocked; perches on roofs; mobs cats and other birds; wobbly flight, with dragging tail; builds big nest in tall tree

loud, rattling *shakashakashaka*

common and widespread, except far north-west Scotland; woodland, farmland, towns, gardens, golf courses

Jay

This intelligent and adaptable bird can live almost anywhere.

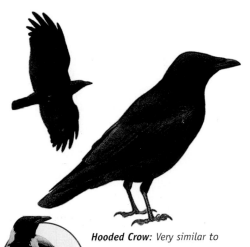

bigger than Magpie; completely black, with powerful bill; young are slightly browner; **black (not bare) base of bill**; in flight, square-ended tail

usually alone or in small groups, but may form flocks; walks or hops on ground; slow, steady flight; eats anything from worms to dead animals; builds big nest in tall tree

deep, cawing *kraaa, kraaa*

very common and widespread, except Ireland and western Scotland (where replaced by Hooded Crow); most rural and urban habitats – especially parks

Rook, Hooded Crow, Raven, Jackdaw, Chough

Hooded Crow: Very similar to Carrion Crow, but with pale grey back and belly; common in Ireland, and north and western Scotland.

A deep croak often lets you know when a raven is about.

biggest crow (bigger than Buzzard); completely black, with massive bill and shaggy throat; in flight, diamond-shaped tail and longer neck than other crows

usually in pairs, but may gather in groups to feed; walks on the ground; in flight, soars like bird of prey and often performs tumbling aerobatics; eats anything from worms and eggs to rabbits and carrion; usually nests on cliffs

deep, hollow-sounding croak, *kronk, kronk*

cliffs, mountains and moorland, mostly in western regions; uncommon, but increasing

Rook, Carrion Crow, Hooded Crow, Chough, large birds of prey

119

Gathering 'crows' in a farmer's field are most likely to be Rooks.

slightly smaller than Carrion Crow, and shaggier, with peaked crown and 'baggy trousers'; glossy black, with purplish sheen; pale **bare patch at base of bill**; in flight, shows clearer 'fingers' than crow, and more rounded tail

usually in large flocks; feeds in fields on grain and worms; often beside roads; nests in colonies (rookeries) at top of tall, bare trees

grating croaks – *graarrr, graarr*; very noisy at rookery

common and widespread, except north-west Scotland; farmland with woods; not city centres

Carrion Crow, Hooded Crow, Raven, Jackdaw, Chough

This neat, upright little crow finds a ready-made rooftop home.

much smaller than Rook, with stocky shape and short bill; blackish-grey, except for **paler grey hood and pale eye**; shorter, more rounded wings than Rook

usually in pairs or flocks; hops on ground or walks fast; gathers with Rooks or Starlings; dives and tumbles in flight (especially around cliffs); nests in holes – including chimneys; visits birdtables

sharp *jack, jack*, and higher-pitched *kyow*

common and widespread, except north-west Scotland; farmland, woodland, towns and villages; likes old buildings and sea-cliffs

Carrion Crow, Hooded Crow, Rook, Chough, Feral Pigeon

Starling (21.5cm)

Waddling starlings squabble at the bird table.

winter

smaller and more upright than Blackbird, with shorter tail and sharper bill; in summer, **oily-black with brownish wings and yellow bill**; speckled in winter; young are greyish-brown, with spotted belly in first winter; in flight, paler, triangular wings

feeds in groups; waddles on ground, probing with bill; waves wings while singing; may roost in thousands; visits feeders and birdbaths; fast, direct flight; huge flocks twist and turn in midair

complicated song with rattles and whistles; imitates anything – from other birds to telephones

common and widespread; power lines, lawns, rubbish dumps, seashore; may roost on bridges, piers or buildings

Blackbird, Jackdaw, Waxwing (rare)

House Sparrow (14–15cm)

The decline of our best-known town bird has puzzled scientists.

small and plump, with short, thick bill; male is streaky chestnut above and pale grey below, with **grey crown and rump**, pale cheeks and black bib; female and young are streaky brown above with pale eyebrow

flocks around buildings; hops on ground; may chase insects in flight; colonies nest on roofs and roost in bushes; winter flocks gather on farmland; straight flight

simple chirps and chirrups

very common and widespread, though declining; always near human activity, such as farms and towns; not forests, mountains or moorland

Tree Sparrow, Dunnock, Chaffinch (female)

♀

♂

This neat finch is one of our three most common birds.

- slimmer than sparrow; pale, pointed bill; male has chestnut back, white wing-bars, **blue-grey head and pink breast and face**; female is more pinkish brown; in flight, white wing-bars, white outer tail feathers and greenish rump

- alone or in pairs; feeds on ground with nodding walk; sings from high perch; flocks with other finches in winter; bouncing flight

- loud *chink-chink* call; song is downward rattle ending in flourish

- very common and widespread; all habitats (often in places with few other birds); parks and gardens

- House Sparrow (female), Brambling

A flock of Goldfinches adds an extra splash of colour to autumn.

- small and agile, with longish bill; sandy brown, with black, white and red face; **black and yellow wings** very clear in flight; young have plain head

- feeds on low plants, such as thistles or dandelions; dangles acrobatically to reach seeds; nests in trees; gathers in large autumn flocks

- simple *twit-a-twit* flight call; long, twittering song – quite similar to Swallow

- common and widespread, except in far north; likes rough, open country, such as wasteland, golf courses and road verges; visits garden feeders

- Greenfinch, Siskin, Linnet

Greenfinch (15cm)

This chunky green-and-yellow finch is a confident visitor to feeders.

sparrow-sized; forked tail; male is mostly bright green; female is duller; **bold yellow markings on wings and tail** show when perched and in flight

feeds on seeds on ground and in trees; circular spring display flight from treetop perch, with slow wingbeats; joins mixed finch flocks in winter; likes feeders

during display, makes loud twittering trill followed by long, wheezy *dzeeeee*; also *chichichi* flight call

common and widespread; woods, gardens and farmland – also along coast during winter

Siskin, Goldfinch, Yellowhammer, House Sparrow (female)

Siskin (12cm)

This lively little finch often behaves more like a blue tit.

smaller than Greenfinch, with narrower bill and nore forked tail; male is streaky green above, with **yellow breast and face, black cap and short black bib**; female is streakier with no black on face; bright yellow wing and tail markings

flocks feed acrobatically in treetops (especially alder and birch) – often with Redpolls; visits garden feeders in early spring

tzeuu or *tzuee* flight call; twittering, wheezing song

breeds mostly in coniferous forests – most common in north and west; widespread in winter in mixed woodland (often near water), parks and gardens

Greenfinch, Lesser Redpoll, Goldfinch

Linnet (13.5cm)

This handsome songster is easiest to identify in spring.

- slim finch, with small bill and forked tail; spring male has **chestnut back, grey head**, red forehead and red patches on breast; otherwise streaky brown, like female; in flight, white patch on primaries and tail

- feeds on or near ground (never in trees), taking seeds from low plants; sings from top of bush; joins mixed finch flocks in winter

- twittering flight call; twittering song, with scratchy and wheezy notes

- common and widespread except in far north; prefers rough open ground – especially with gorse; along coast in winter; seldom visits gardens

- Chaffinch, Redpoll, Twite

♂

♀

Bullfinch (15–16cm)

This colourful finch has a strong bill for plucking buds and seeds.

♀

♂

- plump, with thick neck and thick bill; male has rose-pink face and underparts, black crown, and grey back with pale wing-bar; female has same pattern, but browner and duller; young have plain crown; in flight, **broad white rump**

- secretive and always near cover; feeds in pairs or small groups in trees or low plants; eats seeds and buds; doesn't flock with other finches

- soft, sorrowful *pee-uu* call; quiet song

- widespread, but declining; mixed woodland, farmland with hedgerows, orchards, parks and large gardens

- Chaffinch, Hawfinch, Robin

Look out for a yellow blob on top of a gorse bush.

♂

♀

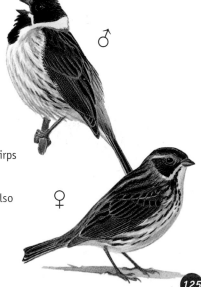

larger than sparrow, with longer tail; breeding male has streaky chestnut back, **yellow head** and streaky yellow breast; female and non-breeding male are duller brown with heavier streaking; in flight, chestnut rump and white outer tail feathers

feeds on ground; sings from top of bush; gathers in mixed winter flocks; dipping flight

grating *zit* call; short song all on one note except for last – *se-se-se-se-se-se-soo*

common and widespread; open country with hedgerows and bushes – especially gorse and hawthorn

Cirl Bunting (rare), Corn Bunting, Reed Bunting, Skylark

Reed Bunting (15cm)

The male's bold black-and-white head stands out among reeds.

sparrow-sized; breeding male has pale underparts, streaky chestnut back and **black head with white collar and moustache**; female and non-breeding male are duller, but with well-marked face; in flight, white outer tail feathers

usually feeds close to water – often among reeds; male sings from bush; forms flocks in winter with finches and pipits

metallic *ching* call; simple song is a few repeated chirps

widespread except in uplands; mostly damp areas, including reedbeds, marshes and waterside scrub; also commons, farmland and young plantations

Yellowhammer, House Sparrow, Tree Sparrow, Lapland Bunting (rare)

♂

♀

Glossary

Albino: white or partly white plumage that is not usually white.

Arable field: a field in which crops are grown.

Auk: a type of diving seabird, such as Guillemot or Puffin.

Bib: a patch of colour on a bird's chin and throat, shaped like a baby's bib.

Bird recorder: a person who keeps official records of birds.

Breeding plumage: a bird's plumage while breeding and preparing to breed (usually early spring to summer).

Brood: young birds hatched from a single clutch of eggs.

Canopy: the top part of a tree or forest, with dense leaves and branches.

Chestnut: reddish-brown, like the colour of horse chestnut (conker).

Clutch: group of eggs laid together in the same nest.

Colony: a group of birds breeding close together.

Cover: an area where you can't easily be seen, such as behind a bush.

Crown: the top part of a bird's head.

Dawn chorus: many birds singing together at the start of a spring day.

Display flight: a special flight that some male birds use to attract females.

Diving duck: a species of duck, such as the Tufted Duck, that feeds mostly by diving under water.

Drumming: the mechanical courtship noise made by a woodpecker banging on a tree or a Snipe vibrating its tail feathers in flight.

Eclipse plumage: a male duck's plumage during moult, when it looks like a female.

Eyepieces: the parts of a telescope or pair of binoculars that you look through.

Feeding party: a mixed group of small birds that get together outside the breeding season to find food.

Feral: descended from a domesticated species, but living wild.

Fieldmark: a special feature of a bird's plumage that helps you to identify it.

Fledgling: a young bird that gets its first adult feathers, ready for flying.

Flush: to cause a bird to fly off by walking too close to it.

Forage: search for food on the ground or among vegetation.

Forewing: the front part of a bird's wing in flight.

Game bird: a type of plump ground bird, such as Pheasant or Red Grouse.

Gravel pit: a hole dug to collect gravel for building, that has been flooded like a lake.

Habitat: any particular type of landscape in which a bird lives, such as woodland or an estuary.

Heathland: a southern lowland habitat, with sandy soil, heather, gorse and bogs.

Hide: a small building from which to watch birds while staying hidden.

High tide line: the highest point that waves reach on a beach, often marked by seaweed.

Host bird: a bird, such as Dunnock, in whose nests Cuckoos lay their eggs.

Identification: working out the name of a bird; sometimes known as ID.

Jizz: the unique character of each bird species that you learn with experience.